"Whatsoever things are...lovely...
think on these things."

PHILIPPIANS 4:8

Whatsoever Things Are Lovely

By
Foy Valentine

2004

Whatsoever Things Are Lovely
By Foy Valentine
Copyright © 2004 by Foy Valentine.
All rights reserved.

Christian Ethics Today Publications
Post Office Box 26
Wimberley, Texas 78676

Multiple copies of this book may be secured from the publisher. Please write for special arrangements.

Published by Scriptum Publishing House
Lapusului 28, 410690 Oradea, Romania. www.scriptum.ro

ISBN 973-85279-5-3

Jacket photograph by Jean Valentine

Typeset and printed by Policontact Ltd. (www.policontact.ro)

National Library of Romania Cataloging-in-Publication Data
VALENTINE, FOY
      Whatsoever Things Are Lovely / Foy Valentine. - Oradea: Scriptum, 2004
      ISBN 973-85279-5-3

To

LAURA, JOHN, TREY, WILL, and CATHERINE,
grandchildren
who impress their grandparents
as being
well above average

CONTENTS

Publisher's preface 9
A Paean for Place 11
A Walk in the Woods..16
Creativity 20
The Ten Most Beautiful Sights in the World...............23
Laughter..27
Don Quixote 31
Fifty Fabulous Things..35
Rocks 39
Ten Things to Light Your Fire....................................44
The Signed Blank Check 49
Diatribe on Cybernetics 52
Sunsets 56
On Being Seventy Five...58
Of She Bears and Y2K 61
The Joy of Eating..66
In Celebration of Fire..72
Dayspring...75
What's the Good Word? 79
The Letter Giveth Life...83
Ten Good Things 87
Wisdom 92
Cars. Cars. Cars. 97

Christmas: Magic and Miracle 102
Change...106
Fishing 110
Turtles Do 114
Sounds of the Season 119
Stoking and Poking 123
Trivial Pursuits...129
Funny How Time Gets Away 134
Summertime..138
Imprecation for an Answering Machine 145
When Ladies at the Lattice Lose Their Luster..............147
The Shade at the End of the Row 152
Ich Glaube än Gott 157

Publisher's preface

HERE IS A DELIGHTFUL book.

It is down to earth.

It is literate.

It is erudite.

It is reverent.

And it is as refreshing as a glass of cold lemonade on a hot summer day.

In 35 short articles, the author shares good-humored, down-home, stream-of-consciousness insights that are incisive and disarmingly candid. The book's silk purses often masquerade as sow's ears.

Dedicated to whimsy, nostalgia, and "things unsubstantive" which the author calls "my specialty," the book could be read at one sitting but is more likely to be relished when read piece by piece at a more leisurely pace.

Originally written over a period of years as essays for the journal *Christian Ethics Today,* which the author founded in 1995, these articles come from the mind and heart of a man who knows very well who he is and who is completely at ease with where he came from.

Proceeds from the book go in their entirety to the Christian Ethics Today Foundation, publisher of the *Christian Ethics Today* journal.

Dr. Foy Valentine, the author, is a graduate of Baylor University with triple majors in Bible, Speech, and English and of Southwestern Baptist Theological Seminary with an earned Doctor of Theology degree and a major in Christian Social Ethics. He worked full-time in the field of Christian ethics for 35 years, first as head of the Texas Baptist Christian Life Commission and then as Director of the Christian Life Commission of the Southern Baptist Convention. A well known and highly respected personality in Baptist life, and beyond, for 50 years, Dr. Valentine is the recipient of distinguished alumni awards from his alma maters, has received a number of honorary doctoral degrees, and is listed in both Who's Who in America and in Who's Who in the World.

He is married to the former Mary Louise Valentine. They have three grown daughters, Jean, Carol, and Susan, and five grandchildren.

A Paean
for Place

PAEAN: A SONG OF praise or exultation.

Place: A portion of space; a definite location; a spot devoted to a specified purpose; an area.

A body is blessed who has a strong sense of place. Knowing the place where we are helps us to know the persons who we are. Also, if we are clear about the place where we have come from , we can better understand the place where we are now, and we can better see the place where we need to be.

Geography's demise is humanity's loss.

In all the history of humanity, there has probably never before been a time when there is as much voluntary migration as there is in the world today. The resulting loss of familiar place tends to bring about disorientation and alienation.

If we belong to no place, we have no bearings. Not to have bearings, not to be oriented to Place and Time, not to exist in relationship to fixed points is, by definition, to be lost.

Part of the punishment borne by Adam and Eve was that they were banished from their Place, driven out by the great God Almighty from the Garden, doomed to dwell East of Eden, displaced.

When Cain had killed his brother Abel, he too was displaced, "driven...away from the ground" to "be a fugitive and a wanderer....away from the presence of the Lord," where he, too, "dwelt in the land of Nod, east of Eden" (Genesis 4:14-16).

My home Place holds such good memories for me that it doesn't even have to be a good day for me to bask in recollections related to it.

Although I lived there only 17 years, from birth until I went away to college, the solidities, realities, specifics, and verities of that Place seem more concrete and more satisfyingly solid as the years go by.

No, we were not upwardly mobile. Nor downwardly mobile. Nor sidewardly mobile. We stayed put. In that Place. As Greenwich in London is the bearing point from which all modern latitudinal and longitudinal measurements and orientations are reckoned the wide world over, so our Place was the only Greenwich I knew anything about from my birth to my Exodus from Edgewood. Our dogs and cats were oriented to that Place. The cows and their calves were oriented to that Place. Even the mules were oriented to that Place for after the Great Depression shifted into overdrive in the early 1930s and the family Ford was sold, our family went about three miles to church every Sunday in a narrow tired wagon pulled by two lively mules, Steve and Red; and you had better believe they knew their way back home to their Place, and ours, without benefit of a $1,000 transponder to bounce signals off a satellite, compute their location, and then provide them with a transistorized display of where they were so that they might then decide where they were and then go home. Thus it becomes crystal clear that Steve and Red were smarter than the thousand dollar option on a new Cadillac. Oh, pretension. And consummate silliness.

Our Place was blessed with a fireplace, and that fireplace in the wintertime conjures up, what else?, my warmest memories. There were roaring fires, glowing coals, hot ashes, cherry red hot andirons, flickering firelight, great oak backlogs, and pleasant, small poppings to toast cold feet, dry out wet britches, banish the chill, and resist the fierce aggressions of the infamous Texas Blue Northers.

The dining room makes that whole Place still smell good in my mind's nose. If my mother had not been such a good cook I might not be a fat man today. The Mother God gave me gave me to eat (as Adam said to the Lord, blaming Him for his sin) and I did eat, and eat, and eat--hot biscuits and gravy, fried chicken, fresh pork ribs, coconut pie, and so on and so forth.

The porches of that Place pleasured me. There was a fine, long porch across the entire front of the house. A big L-shaped back porch at the back of the house domiciled a massive old ice box (the kind you stored great chunks of ice in, chopped from the tank in the wintertime), an old tin safe, an adjoining cistern from which we drew our drinking water, and a pleasant corner in which boys in the summertime could luxuriate in a few buckets of water in Number Two washtubs. Well, where else do you think we could have performed our ablutions? Nobody had bathrooms inside the house for heaven's sake. Nobody had running water. Nobody had electricity. Nobody had nothing. We are talking Early Primitive.

I liked my upstairs bedroom Place. I had it all to myself for five years after my brother went away to college. Thought he never would clear out. I slept with the windows open most of the time. The great magnolia tree's blooms fragranced the Place, the strong clear call of the whip-poor-wills were more soothing to the ears than the 10 o'clock news and Jay Leno put together, and frequent visitations of startlingly loud hoot owls signaled that there was out there in the dark a whole nother world.

I especially relish the memory of the trees of that Place: great old post oaks (still there and probably at least two hundred years old by now), some blackjacks, elms, a wonderful big hickory, the magnolia, crape myrtles, some hackberries; and the big fig tree from which my mother made mouth-watering fig preserves which won the blue ribbons at the annual Van Zandt County Fairs, and under which one pleasant Sunday morning there coiled a territorially jealous copperhead snake that, when I stepped under the tree to gather figs, unceremoniously bit me, apparently without a qualm, and very nearly killed me; and, a quarter of a mile away there were the woods themselves with squirrels, possums, bees, bird nests, little saplings (to be climbed and ridden to the ground by little saps), and big trees to be chopped partly down by my father with a double bit axe and then felled by my brother and me with a two-man cross cut saw. (In this context, a "two-person" cross cut saw would strike me as being just a shade too much, the gender revolution notwithstanding—"pedantic effrontery up with which I will not put," as Winston Churchill is said to have said). Anyhow, what did you think we used to cut fire wood and stove wood with? A big, shiny, yellow McCullough chain saw? They hadn't been dreamed of; gasoline was not available; and there was no money. No problem. We cut the wood. Fine and dandy.

I liked the tank at our Place. It was big and deep, especially at the south end near the dam. And it was splendidly peopled with channel catfish for trotlines, bullfrogs for symphonies of incomparably memorable, altogether pleasant, bass croaking that still rings in my significantly challenged auditory nerves.

And I liked the barn. The barn was very special at our Place. A small body could swing by his arms from rafter to rafter, from one crib to another, then across the whole loft, and then back again. The scent of the hay and the corn, the delicious feel of tumbling in the cottonseed bin, and the smell, not really good and not really bad, of the cows and horses and chickens and geese and an occasional brood sow, brought inside the barn when she was ready to make her marvelous birthing bed of shucks and straw and find her pigs--all these come vividly to mind.

So, I call this squib a Paean for Place. I exult in such measure of orientation as I have because of my experience with this Place where I grew up. And I hope you are disposed to consider such Place or Places as may be personally meaningful, restorative, even redemptive to you.

It helps to reckon your position now and then, to determine again your bearings, to "look to the rock whence you were hewn...to the...pit whence you were digged" (Isaiah 51:1).

It can be a spiritually enriching, psychically steadying exercise. The fear of the Lord is the beginning of wisdom; and knowing who you are comes in a close second. And Place is very special in helping you know who you are.

A Walk
in the Woods

TODAY I TOOK a walk in the woods.

It was a splendid tonic.

I drove sixty miles to my boyhood home in East Texas, parked the car near a clump of tickle-tongue trees, and moseyed down the long country lane from where our barn used to be to our patch of woods. Those woods are situated in the northwest corner of the property my parents bought for $100 per acre about 80 years ago. That price included the two-story, four bedroom house where I was born, a big barn, an ample shed for a car, a wagon, tools and farm implements, a henhouse, a smokehouse, a cistern, a well, and several remarkably fine neighbors.

But the woods themselves on this pleasant early spring day, were the locus of my ecstasy. There were black jack oaks, post oaks, pin oaks, elms, persimmons, cedars, hickories, ash, and a big thicket of huckleberries. The land itself was partly sandy knolls and partly flat little glades given to retaining rainfall and domiciling crawfish.

The best thing about this walk in the woods was not the walk, of course, but rather:

➤ Sitting a spell on a fallen log encrusted with old shelf lichen, inhabited desultorily by some unaggressive, big wood ants, mutilated by woodpeckers in search of luscious grubs, and still partially clad by decaying slabs of bark ready, in the fullness of time, to fall to the ground at the slightest provocation of a scampering squirrel or a raucous bluejay;

➢ Kneeling on a bed of dry leaves to brush away the winter's accumulated detritus to find nestled under the protecting cover a marvelous little sprig of fern sending out tentative but hopeful little fronds in search of sunlight to activate its astoundingly complex and, to me, miraculous chlorophyll;

➢ Stopping dead-still to marvel at the cottontail rabbit brought to a timorous freeze by my long, low whistle, an un-rabbitlike sound that required it to be still and take inventory of this unexpected presence with this unnatural sound;

➢ Looking up to see a lone buzzard leisurely riding the thermals that neither he nor I could see but that we both could accept with such wonder and gratitude as either of us could muster;

➢ Walking up on some scattered bones, bleached white as cotton by winter wind and summer sun, the final resting place of some cow who had bellied down in the grass never again to summon the strength to get up, on her hind legs first and then on her front legs, for a continuation of her lifelong quest for more grass to put away in one of her many-chambered stomachs before regurgitating it as a cud on which she might placidly chew, as such ruminants are wont to do; or it could have been a small horse unable for that last time to get up, first on its front legs and then on its hind legs, as such creatures do who neither part the hoof nor chew the cud. There was no skull to enable me to make a positive identification of this corpus delicti; but pondered long there in sober reflection on the fleeting nature of life for all creatures great and small which, as James says, is "a vapor that appeareth for a little time and then vanisheth away" (James 4:14);

➤ Spying a not unfriendly brown thrush which, although it is rather secretive by nature, in this instance hopped around in a bush apparently oblivious to my intrusion about which it, at the moment, seemed to be perfectly unconcerned;

➤ Marveling at a squirrel's nest situated precariously on a smallish limb far up in a great old post oak tree which, in the south side of the main trunk, boasted a smoothly worn hole about as big as a hen egg, a hole which no doubt had been stocked by the resident fox squirrel with a goodly supply of acorns;

➤ A mysterious small patch of recently excavated holes whose builders and makers I could not identify but who, I mused, might be foxes, armadillos, civet cats, or some critter totally unknown to me when I first started walking those woods 75 years ago;

➤ A patch of second-growth timber, several acres in all, which brought vivid recollections of the winter when my father decided to clear that land with a sharp double-bit axe, which clearing he did single-handedly, and which virgin land he then broke with two mules and a turning plow before planting a crop of corn and then in due time gathering in the new produce; but this new-ground has now, after sixty-five or seventy years, reverted to its original status without so much as a remaining furrow to mark my father's prodigious labors, which must be something of a parable of all human endeavors from the Hanging Gardens of Semiramis to the Colossus of Rhodes; and coming up on an old snake skin shed when some fearsome, though non-poisonous, black racer had come to its seasonal change of clothing, a mute reminder that the cycles of nature, ordained by the Creator, are moving right along, thank you, no matter who is in the State House, the White House, or the Glass House on the East River and totally oblivious to genomes, space stations, spy planes, or Wall Street gyrations. Hm-m-m-m.

In due time I ambled back to my car by the tickle-tongue trees and relished a peaceful drive back home, breaking the journey only briefly for a Dairy Queen Blizzard dutifully held upside down by the pleasant young woman who had created this luscious concoction before she passed it to me for appropriate disposition, a fitting finale for a wonderful walk in the woods.

Creativity

❧   ❧

J. R. R. TOLKIEN WAS SITTING in his study at Oxford correcting a student's thesis. The year was 1926. For some reason, the student had turned in a blank page. When Tolkien came to it, he picked up his pen and wrote on the page, "In a hole in the ground there lived a hobbit," thus launching one of the more remarkable literary careers of our time. On being asked why he did it, Tolkien replied, "It popped into my head."

No amount of technology can pop something into your head.

No machine can produce a single truly creative act. No matter how advanced or intricate or complex our computers, we remember that they are really nothing more than adding machines, state-of-the-art adding machines to be sure but adding machines just the same, jazzed up abacuses. They can print out only those choices that some intelligent creator has programmed in. Dot-dash, plus-minus, yes-no, black-white, whatever.

In creativity, there is joy and excitement, promise and prospect. In the process of the original creation, the Creator kept making things about which he kept joyously saying, "It is good."

Parents marvel in awe and wonder as they hold their new baby, a creature made in their own image, after their own likeness--the fingers, the toes, the eyes, the flailing arms, the kicking legs, the voice, especially the voice, "Heaven help us; there is that VOICE already in the wee, small hours of the night. What on earth have we created?"

The preacher feels splendidly emptied at the end of a Spirit-blessed sermon.

The author feels gloriously peaceful when the article or book or poem is finally finished and put to bed.

The gardener finds deep pleasure in her orderly rows, her growing radishes, her tasseling corn, her ripening tomatoes.

The artist is wonderfully released from the compulsion that has been driving him on when the last brush stroke is made on the painting.

The musician rests in peace when the concert has gone flawlessly and the last curtain call has been acknowledged.

The cook savors with great satisfaction a meal remembered, course by course, that turns out just exactly right.

Creativity is God-like.

Stiflers of creativity, however, abound on every hand. They are nay-sayers, joy-killers, status quo defenders. Truth is they are anti-Christ's.

Materialism leads the pack. The heavy hand of mammon presses down hard on the free spirit of creativity; but authentic faith points the way to deliverance. Creativity beckons for us to cut the umbilical cord that ties us to business as usual and bids us ride light in the saddle, living up to our high calling as God's Exodus people on our way to the City of God.

Conservatism also hath its terrors. The inclination to conserve the creativities of the past can become such a compelling obsession that nothing new can ever pop into our heads. One of the tragedies of fundamentalism, religious or political or social, is that it is a joyless, argumentative, dogmatic, quarrelsome, fighting neurosis that squelches freedom and quenches creativity. The Devil of fundamentalism scowls and frowns and complains and opposes and bickers and moans and maneuvers and manipulates and schemes and plots but seems incapable of achieving the freedom to enjoy a hearty laugh. Revealed religion, we bear in mind, calls for creativity as well as conservation.

Hedonism comes to mind. The search for new nerve endings to stimulate is an ultimately futile exercise. Chasing after the bright elusive butterfly of pleasure is a sorry summum bonum for creatures made in the image and after the likeness of the great God Almighty. Limits to appetite are found all too quickly when the creative impulse is turned inward to sensate impulses. An antidote is self-giving love.

Creativity can, of course, be stifled. Poverty, too much work, not enough work, injustice, harassment, crowding, noise, loneliness, sickness, hunger, and frustration can all contribute to the smothering of our creative impulses. Both the individual and society have a stake in resisting these stiflers. By resisting, we can provide creativity a chance to help us to mount up with wings as eagles, to run and not be weary, to walk and not faint.

A small note is support of common sense might not be out of place. By creativity I do not mean to champion the bizarre, a Martha Stewart kind of creativity with elegant dining table centerpieces made out of dried horse apples and corncobs sprayed with purple paint, garnished with liver loaf and sprinkled with nutmeg. No. To be creative is not to be off the wall but to be out of the box. For God's sake.

Creativity is God-like.

I wanted to say it.

Besides, it popped into my head.

The Ten Most Beautiful Sights in the World

❧ ❧

FIXED INDELIBLY IN our mind's eyes are certain splendid sights. It pleasures us to lean back, shut our eyes, and remember them in living color. Those sights accumulated across a lifetime can be better than money in the bank. By far.

So, would you pull up a chair and humor me a couple of minutes.

I am remembering the ten most beautiful sights I have ever seen. Hold it just a minute while I get this tired old projector focused. Now.

➢ There is *the black sand beach of Kalapana.* On Hawaii's Big Island before Kilauea blew its top pouring vast quantities of molten lava on it, this was the prettiest place in the world. The exquisite crescent beach was lined with coconut palms; and the bay's great waves ceaselessly pounded and agitated the old black lava to make the fantastic, glistening jet black sand. The perfectly white foam, the navy blue water, the huge turtles wallowing in the surf, and the blue blue sky combined to create what Pele could cover up but what the volcano goddess could never dim from memory.

➢ I remember *Tahiti in the dawn's early light.* One of the most breathtakingly beautiful sights on earth with turquoise water, coral sand, Moorea in the distance, frond-thatched Polynesian shacks in the foreground, and the magic combination of light and color that enraptured and captured French Impressionist artists, English writers, and everybody with a pulse who has ever come near.

➤ Unforgettable are *Northern New Mexico's aspen-covered mountains in October's full color,* vast garments of 24-karat gold. There is simply nothing in this world more gloriously marvelous. No bluer skies on earth, no vaster expanses of delicious solid gold forests, no grander vistas are to be found anywhere in the world that I know of.

➤ Then there is *Lake Louise.* With the glacier feeding it, the Canadian Rocky mountains surrounding it, and the season's first magic snowfall gracing it, Lake Louise lives splendidly in memory. The Banff National Park is Canada's finest treasure; and Lake Louise is the Crown Jewel. Sell all you have and go see it before God calls you home. Heaven probably has more splendid sights; but from here, I cannot for the life of me imagine what they could be like.

➤ Consider *bluebonnets in the Texas Hill Country.* Specifically, just a few miles north of Fredericksburg on a peaceful little black-topped ranch road, a body drives slowly around a bend and over a hill to see an astoundingly beautiful great blue lake in the distant valley and stops to drink it in only then to see that this is not a lake at all. It is an unbelievable expanse of exquisite bluebonnets. Defying description, here is God's special gift not just to Texas and to Texans but to anybody and everybody with eyes to see. This is a first magnitude, world class memory to take with you to that Fair Land Beyond the River.

➤ Think a moment of *the Muir Woods.* California's best gift to the world is this patch of giant redwoods towering to fantastic heights, graced by a little stream brimming with great old ocean weary salmon coming home to spawn, streaked by light shining through the giant trees as in the hush of a great cathedral. This is one of the most fabulous places in all of God's great creation.

➢ Nothing could ever erase, or even fade in the mind's eye, *Ireland's forty shades of green.* Defying description, these undulating green hills are somehow deeply therapeutic. Embellished with fencerows of profusely blooming fuchsia, blackberries ripening in wild exuberance, and a technologically challenged landscape that has hardly changed since St. Patrick first laid eyes on it, Ireland's forty shades of green is a sight that blesses the beholder with wondrously curative special powers.

➢ Fabulous is the word for *Teheran in the desert night.* With a full moon coming up over the Elburz Mountains, with every light in this great city twinkling in the desert air as if to outtwinkle all the others, and with the 18,600 foot peak of Mount Demavent looming distantly in the northeast, the wonder of 1001 Arabian nights engulfs you. Even the angels hush their singing.

➢ *The Taj Mahal.* No human construction compares in beauty to this exquisite monument. Built in Agra, India by the Shah Jahan for his wife, Mumtaz Mahal, the Taj Mahal is unique in conception, design, execution, and impact. I have seen it in the early morning, at high noon, in the late afternoon, and by moonlight. And I would like to see its white marble, its four graceful minarets, its fabled reflection pool, and its exquisite garden surrounded by the red sandstone wall—all—again and again and again.

➢ Queen of the Alps and Mother Superior of all the mountains in all the world, *the Jungfrau* stands splendidly in a class all by itself. The Jungfrau's symmetry, understated grandeur, class, and framing of Interlaken's bright blooms and fine green lawns, combine to showcase the best that the Swiss Alps have to offer in glaciers, ice, pristine snow, and dazzling whiteness.

I also remember Kilimanjaro in the moonlight, the Matterhorn in the morning, rhododendrons covering North Carolina's Mount Mitchell, the sunsets from my boyhood home, of course, and a hundred more. But I have to cease and desist lest, to quote Macbeth, "the line stretch out to the crack of doom."

Why not make your own list? Then when you need a break, flash them on the screen of your mind.

It could be a very religious thing to do.

Epiphanies are for those with eyes to see.

"Whatsoever things are...lovely...think on these things."

Laughter

WHAT COULD BE more lovely than a good belly laugh?

Even a nice little chuckle is not to be sneezed at.

And a good joke is better than a hundred jeremiads. You know, those organ recitals in which operations are enumerated, wrongs are recalled, and troubles are mournfully rehashed.

Not to labor the point unduly, consider the considerable benefits of mirth.

Humor, it seems to me, is God's great gift to a species prone to failure, misery, depression, wrath, remorse, sickness, disease, gout, cataracts, the common cold, war, cruelty, cancer, poverty, pain, exploitation, prejudice, hunger, pride, failure, misery, abuse, torture, violence, and death. If you ask me, who could laugh in the face of such adversities, then I would like to ask you, who could keep his head above water at all without the life raft of laughter to cling to in all those wild waters?

Here, then, is a salute to laughter.

Laughter may well derive from our having been made in the likeness of God. He worked six days in creation, you know, and then washed his hands good and took the next day off. Sitting down he propped up his feet, surveyed his handiwork, and with a broad smile, allowed that it was good. Who knows but that he may have laughed out loud at the ludicrous hippopotamus, at the antics of the monkey, and at *ha adam*, the adam, hairless, teetering around on two legs, and naked as a jaybird?

And we can well imagine that God smiled at the light, at the dry land, at violets, at ripe peaches, at fleecy clouds, at the blue sky, at the fantastic fire he had kindled in the sun, at the splendor of the full moon rising, at the sunset, and at "the stars also" (Genesis 1:16).

Common folk wisdom would have us believe that a spoonful of sugar makes the medicine go down. Actually, I can't quite see it. Still the wise seer of Proverbs 17:22 allowed that "a merry heart doeth good like a medicine." The Psalmist has said that a body who loves righteousness and hates wickedness, that is, a person who has his moral head screwed on reasonably straight is anointed by the Lord "with the oil of gladness" (Psalms 45:7). The author of Hebrews had hid this word about "the oil of gladness" in his, or her, heart (Hebrews 1:9), right up front. Well-being, the peace that passes understanding, the smile that turns easily into laughter are "the oil of gladness" that is the natural corollary of righteousness.

It is always a good day for me when Warren Hultgren, my friend of fifty years, calls me long distance for a leisurely visit. He is fun. His disposition is sunny. He is consistently pleasant. He is upbeat. And I could never ever tell you how many of his stories, yarns, jokes, frivolities, artful exaggerations, and ludicrous little lies, we have, together, laughed at uproariously. Nowadays, I can be driving down the highway all by myself and still burst out laughing at one of his tales which he told me twenty years ago. That tale, I estimate has been worth a minimum of $50,000 to me.

My warm friendship of a lifetime shared with Charles Trentham had such a dimension. Just before he died recently in a terrible car accident, we had occasion to revel together in this tale: it seems that this young preacher was called to two churches on the same day. Not knowing which one to take, but being quite sure that he wanted out of where he was, he went to his old mentor, saying, "What shall I do? I just want, in my ministry, to be where God is." The old pastor said. "That's easy, son. Go where the money is. God is everywhere." I can still hear his deep, resonant, contagious laugh. (If you won't tell anybody, I'll tell you that I told that at his funeral; and I'm pretty sure he relished it again.)

My Texas Aggie brother, Jim, older by five years, and I often call each other long distance to share a small joke, a funny story, a nice turn of phrase, or, rarely, a new blockbuster of humor which simply will not wait until we with mutually advancing auditory challenges (that is French for deafness), can shout it at one another, face to face.

Another friend, Ross Coggins, lights up my whole life with his unique gift of seeing the funny side of things so that any conversation we can manage to have, in person, by phone, or in writing, is a benediction to me, a truly good word.

Laughter's universal appeal is clearly seen in my friend Bruce McIver's phenomenally popular *Stories I Could Not Tell While I Was A Pastor*, a funny book now in its twelfth printing and recently released, together with its sequel, *Just As Long As I'm Riding Up Front*, by *Guideposts* as their featured Spring promotion on a national and international scale.

You can understand why I feel compelled to rise up and call these people blessed. They have employed laughter to our mutual edification, made life's rough places a little smoother, for a little while enabled us to soar above the rough terrain through which we have been stumbling, and obliterate for the moment the nagging pain, the miserable failures, and the everlasting thorns in the flesh which, if allowed to do so, would drain the juices of our souls, gnaw at our spirits, and consume us all.

So...

Smile. It beats frowning.

Chuckle. It beats grouching.

Laugh. It beats crying.

Laughter. Let's celebrate it and thank God for it. It is a lovely thing.

Don Quixote

NOW AND THEN, say every 500 years or so, some genius invents an immortal.

Homer did it with Ulysses.

Some pale Scandinavian did it with Beowulf.

Bunyan did it with Pilgrim.

Some quintessential Englishman did it with King Arthur.

And Cervantes—let the drums roll—did it with Don Quixote.

More real in fiction than most people are in real life, Don Quixote is known and embraced around the world. He is more popular now than when he first sprang onto the world stage 400 years ago.

For instance, on my own desk there stands a 12-inch high wood carving of this worthy Knight of the Rueful (Read Sad, Pitiable, Mournful, Squalid) Countenance. Astride his pitiful old nag (spavined, undernourished, rib cage exposed, abused, and dispirited), the man of La Mancha bears in his right hand his ludicrous overlong lance, disports his silly armor which he has scavenged, wears his absurd helmet which he and Sancho Panza have improvised from a hapless barber's abandoned wash basin, and gazes earnestly into space as he awaits his next outlandish new adventure.

If the famous artist in Mexico, none other than J. Pinal himself, who sold us this masterpiece could only have known what pleasure his handiwork would afford me, he could have got away with charging Mary Louise ten times as much as she paid for it. So be it. Let the seller beware.

On my study wall there hangs a really good oil painting, also from Mexico City and also by a famous artist, of Don Quixote and Sancho Panza on their mounts, Don Quixote on Rocinante and Sancho on the ass. They are making their way through deep woods. Sancho is clearly ready for a square meal and a good night's sleep and Don Quixote is clearly ready to do the noble work of a knight-errant, rescuing some damsel in distress, avenging some injustice, or righting some dastardly wrong. Ethics at its best. (So there. You thought I'd never find a handle to justify all this meandering, didn't you? Ethics, I must remind you, is my calling.)

And hard by, in my work room, there hangs Picasso's striking rendition, in garish red, of—who else—Don Quixote.

Moreover a Broadway musical about the Man of La Mancha has recently been wildly popular.

And a song based on Don Quixote's life, "The Impossible Dream," has been sung by millions and has possibly inspired ten times that many sermons, many of them eminently sleep-worthy, to be sure.

Indeed, this Don Quixote is ubiquitous.

And well he should be.

Consider his credentials.

Cervantes, whose full and proper name was Miguel de Cervantes Saavedra, was born in Alcla de Henares, Spain in 1547 and died at age 69 in 1616. He began giving Don Quixote to the world and to the ages in 1604 and 1605. The second part of the book appeared toward the end of 1615. Written some ten years after the first part, the second part is considered better, more subtle, more stylistically excellent, more focused, more logical, more structured, and more mature than the earlier part. But from beginning to end, the book is stamped indelibly with Cervantes' genius. To read the English translation is to be absolutely astounded with Cervantes' imagination and seemingly inexhaustible vocabulary; and those whose mother tongue is Spanish assure me that when reading it in the Spanish which Cervantes employed, Don Quixote is even more astonishingly remarkable for its vocabulary and glowing realism, its sympathetic insight into the everyday lives of nobles, knights, priests, traders, shepherds, farmers, innkeepers, muleteers, convicts, kitchen workers, ladies, damsels, Moorish beauties, country girls, and kitchen wenches of easy virtue.

Don Quixote has always pleased the multitudes because of its fast pace, its uncomplicated comedy, its kindly pathos, its delicious absurdities, its generous humanity, its spontaneous gaity, its ingenious wit, and its penetrating insight into real life.

Hardly any knowledgeable critic would hesitate to name Cervantes, on the basis of Don Quixote alone, one of history's greatest writers. A much used observation has been that children lovingly turn its pages, young people avidly read it, adults never tire of it, and old people continue to delight in it.

The character of Don Quixote himself is an inexhaustible mine for students and scholars, a treasure trove of psychological studies and theological insights, and a mother lode of plain common sense and authentic wisdom.

That Don Quixote himself is crazy as a loon only serves to make people identify with him all the more sympathetically.

He appeals to me, and in turn I commend him to you for several reasons.

He has a passionate desire to do ethics.

He dreams the impossible dream.

He does not count the cost in pursuing justice.

He wears his authentic humanity honestly.

He relates to Sancho decently and fairly.

He has courage, even to tilt at windmills.

He knows the Bible and often quotes it.

He can laugh at himself.

He is tireless in his pursuit of the good.

He loves words and is unfailingly loquacious.

He employs a vocabulary that would fell a water buffalo at 100 yards.

He is often funny enough to make a dog laugh.

He is gloriously literate.

He is the kind of chap who would seem to me to want his chili hot, his heroes human, and the truth with the bark on it.

Besides all this, to tell the truth, the old codger just seems to me to be quite a lot like my kind of folks.

Let's hear it for Don Quixote.

Fifty
Fabulous Things

HAVING DILLY DALLIED, procrastinated, sublimated, postponed, and otherwise chomped at the bits as long as I could stand it, I proposed marriage to Mary Louise on our second date. (I've always had this problem with making up my mind. A character flaw, I suppose. Or maybe a defective gene.) After two years, she quickly accepted. On May 6, 1947 we were married.

Late in the year as we approached 1997, the year of our Fiftieth Anniversary, our darling daughters began to make dire and dreadful noises. They thought of celebrating this big event with a rip-roaring gala. We reacted violently. They offered us a splendid reception. We couldn't see it. They asked us to consider a big to-do at church. We demurred.

On our own initiative late that year, we devised our very own Grand Scheme to celebrate this Fiftieth Anniversary. We decided to do Fifty Fabulous Things. And thereby hangs this tale. Please draw up a chair and come in close so we can share some of the highlights from those Fifty Fabulous Things which are all now a fait accompli (as are we, for all practical purposes.)

The Faberge Collection. We caught that show in New Orleans. Mary Louise wanted to see the do-dads and I wanted to see what another French Huguenot had wrought, he as an enterprising operator in the shadow of the Kremlin while my own Huguenot forebears were hewing out a new

life on the wild frontier in America. Although I really
hadn't planned to, I enjoyed the display. Mary Louise loved
it. We had a great hotel room looking down on a fine bend
in the mighty Mississippi. Then there were eminently
memorable meals at Brennans and at the Commander's
Palace which topped that cake.

*The 150th Anniversary Celebration of the First Baptist
Church of Gonzales, Texas.* This experience can only be
described as glorious. From beginning to end. Mary Louise
and I had lived there in their parsonage for three years,
1950-1953, for what we now perceive to have been the three
happiest years of our lives. The old friends, evidences of
God's grace, precious memories, warm hospitality,
outstanding programs, and Pastor Brad Russell's generous
invitation for me to preach the Anniversary Sermon
combined to make that a Five Star Happening.

The Fixing of Our Front Yard. This was the special gift of
our children who gave us a landscape beautification face-lift
for the small front yard of our ten-year-old zero-lot line
house, complete with splendid stone work, pink azaleas,
beautiful shrubs, and hundreds upon hundreds of seasonal
flowers. Somewhat breathtaking.

The Reunion of Our Clan. We gathered at the river, at Red
River, New Mexico, to be exact, where we have a homemade
red fir cabin which I built in 1958 with two carpenters and
my own two cotton-picking hands in two weeks (nobody
can figure how we spent that much time on it), where the
altitude is 9500 feet, the distance to the trout stream is ten
feet, the temperature at night is nearly always in the 30's
even in August, the 1946 Willys Jeep always starts, good

pinon fires blaze cheerily every morning and every night, and the columbines bloom profusely among the blue spruce and aspen trees. There our whole family, every last one of them, came in for a couple of weeks of noisy, happy, hungry, hyper togetherness. There were white water raftings, jeep trips, and climbs to Wheeler Peak (the highest mountain in New Mexico) and to Gold Hill (at timberline and right above Goose Lake). There were picnics, cookouts, hikes into the Rio Grande Box Canyon, birthday celebrations, homemade ice cream feasts, after-supper wild animal safaris, and I don't know what all. (It all runs together when you're having that much fun.) This was the most fantastic of our Fifty Fabulous Things. It is preserved for us in the outstanding family portraits and pictures taken in our front yard by professional photographer, par excellence, Carl Brown. He took 89 marvelous pictures all of which were good and the best of which are now in an oversize montage in one frame hanging on our bedroom wall to our daily delight.

Colonial Williamsburg. Who could gild this lily? Mary Louise and I reveled in the Inn itself, its wonderful food, beautiful music, superior staff, excellent accommodations, homey ambiance, and Colonial atmosphere. We liked it more than any place we've ever been. Now, we can think of no place we had rather return to or go to again if we could do it all over. Williamsburg is the creme de la creme of our Fifty Fabulous Things.

England. Having accumulated more than 200,000 Frequent Flyer miles, we flew first class and free from Dallas to London and back in September. Four days in London were highlighted by Oliver (the best play we've seen in years), visits with old friends, and an unhurried visit to the British Museum. Four days in the Cotswolds pleasured us with thatch roofed houses, delightful English gardens, and pleasant outings. Several days in Wales at Lord Ashley's Jacobean era (1652) small hotel in a room decorated by Laura Ashley herself, overlooking the River Wye were highlighted by sumptuous meals and vividly memorable walks in their fruited and flowering gardens. Several days in the Lake District in a small hotel over-looking Lake Windermere were—what can I say?—fabulous. (Oh, England is a perfect place to lose pounds—pounds sterling, that is.)

There was much, much more. Our minds race back to bluebonnets in the Texas Hill Country, the Fantastics, Bed and Breakfasts, our cousin's Sixtieth Wedding Anniversary Celebration in their sweet potato curing barn at Edgewood, raspberry preserve making, the good news that our oldest grandchild had been admitted to start to Baylor in the next fall, paying off our house mortgage, the happy completion of negotiations for the Center for Christian Ethics at Baylor University, uncounted encounters with hot cornbread and banana puddings, the full color of Virginia's autumn foliage, and some 207 games of Scrabble including weekly knock-down-and-drag-outs with old friends Darold and Elizabeth Morgan.

You get the drift. We liked it. And, we commend some such splendid foolishness to any and all who can screw their courage to the sticking point and do it.

The golden Anniversary Year for Mary Louise and me is now spent. Our energy is spent. Our money is spent. And we ourselves are pooped but proud. The experience has been "altogether lovely" and we now tiredly but happily "think on these things."

Rocks

❧   ☙

A FEW SHRIVELED souls I know are not crazy about rocks.

They are to be pitied.

The depths of their deprivation boggles the mind.

If good manners allowed, they should be discreetly shunned.

As for me, I just love rocks.

Always have.

At least I can't remember a time when I was not smitten by rocks, charmed by rocks, enthralled by rocks, fascinated by rocks.

Where I grew up as a boy in East Texas, there were no rocks. Oh, there may have been some deep down in the earth; but where I lived, God covered them all up with fine sandy loam and immense deposits of splendid red clay.

I was, well, rock challenged.

When I went away to college at Baylor, I was drawn, like a moth to a flame, to a geology class. It was love at first sight. I was so pleasured with all those glorious rocks that I knocked the top out of the curve in that class, much to the consternation of the several geology majors in the class. I meant them no harm. It was just that I couldn't help myself. I liked geology so much that I pretty nearly ate it with a spoon. I loved it with an agape kind of love, as everybody in church now says...especially those who don't know Greek. No matter that I had a triple major in Bible and English and Speech, I would gladly have added a geology major too if my meager resources had allowed.

Since college, my work has taken me on travels far and wide and I have hardly ever gone anywhere in the world without bringing back some wonderful rock as a memento. There are hundreds of these fantastic treasures. Altogether they could not possibly be worth thirty cents. But by each, there hangs some marvelous tale.

Let me illustrate.

Here on my desk is an ammonite, a limestone fossil some 200 million years old which our Number One grandson, John, and I chiseled out of a deposit of fossiliferous limestone from a dry creek bed behind our house. What a wonder.

On the corner of my desk is a rock I gouged out of the stony bank completely encircling the town of Nordlingen in southern Germany. When that area was a very shallow sea covered with primordial muck, a huge meteor came swooshing in, at some two or three thousand miles per hour, made a great splash and a huge crater which subsequently filled in so that the marvelous little Bavarian city in due season could be neatly built in it, and the surrounding wall was thrown up in an instant, in a perfect circle. My fist-sized rock is composed of hundreds, maybe thousands of tiny sea shells which come into fascinating focus under a strong magnifying glass. It is enough to elicit a hallelujah chorus, with trumpet flourishes no less.

Then there is this piece of jasper which I picked up at the very top of Wheeler Peak, the highest mountain in New Mexico. As one of the highest mountains of the Sangre de Christo (Blood of Christ) Range, it yielded from its very summit this glorious bloodred piece of jasper. The rock was a thing of beauty before my brother Jim, a devoted rock hound, polished it to perfection. It is now exquisite.

I particularly like this aa, a broken and jagged chunk of black lava from a recent eruption of Kilauea on Mauna Loa's leeward side on the big island of Hawaii. It has a yellowish tinge and still smells of sulphur, which the ancients, with good cause, called brimstone. And just think: it comes from the side of the biggest mountain on earth which from the bottom of the Pacific to its snow-covered peak is some 32,000 feet. Now that is a pile of rocks.

Good memories are attached to this smooth stone which I picked up at the very end of the Kenai Peninsula in Alaska at the uttermost tip of the North American land mass, hard by some calving glaciers. It still feels a little cold.

Then there is this small piece of basalt which some straw-hatted laborer long, long ago worked into the Great Wall of China. I honored him, I recall, as I walked in awe along the top of his handiwork, the only human construct which the early astronauts could make out from their orbits in outer space.

The red coral piece comes from the beach at Bali in Indonesia. I picked it up at sunset. What a memorable walk; what a view; and what a rock.

The ten-pound stone, black but chock full of small white fossils, I found in the Rocky Mountains where one shifting tectonic plate pushed another plate up from sea-level to 12,000 feet, a little while ago. To get my specimen to its present round, smooth, and beautiful shape required quite a vast amount of time and tumbling which it would take a Jules Verne on peyote to conjure up.

Time would fail me to tell

➢ Of the small rectangular stone which the Roman Emperor Hadrian had his workmen incorporate into a 73″ mile sentry beat, Hadrian's Wall, across northern

England to keep the savage Norse invaders out of the then only slightly less savage Roman province of Britain,

➤ Of the cannon-ball sized piece of quartz with moss still on it which I found recently on the banks of the River Wye in Wales,

➤ Of the small smooth flint rock I found in Israel like one David could have fitted into his sling shot for , as his faithless detractors imagined, his foolhardy face-off with Goliath,

➤ Of the piece of one of the great pyramids of Egypt which some ego-crazed Pharaoh ordered as a memorial for his own royal, he believed divine, self,

➤ Of the old slate shingle which some rustic mountain man long ago fashioned with his ancient zax, for a part of a roof for his cowshed in the shadow of Switzerland's Matterhorn just a short walk outside of Zermatt,

➤ Of the shiny chunk of mica I picked up in Colorado while waiting to ship home the body of my good friend, Charles Trentham, killed in a tragic car wreck on his way to our cabin in Red River, New Mexico,

➤ Of the fist-sized chunk of conglomerate composed of pure white coral sand and coal black lava pebbles ground down by a pounding Pacific surf on the windward side of Kauai to a perfect goose-egg shape,

➤ And of the neat paving stone from the Appian Way just outside the city of Rome with the marks of a thousand Roman chariots well worn into the surface.

I really want to go on and on.
But I have to stop.
Every rock holds the memories of a lifetime. Too, as Shakespeare in *As You Like It* has the Duke to say about the good life in Arden Forest, there are "books in the running

brooks, sermons in stones, and good in everything." Indeed, there are "sermons in stones." Although I'm sorely tempted, I'll refrain from preaching them since this essay is dedicated to whimsy and things unsubstantive. My specialty.

No wonder Chevrolet has stuck with its immensely successful sales pitch, "Like a rock. Um-m-m. Like a rock."

And especially no wonder that our great and wonderful God who is himself the Rock of Ages is also the Rock of our salvation.

Hooray for rocks.

Ten Things
to Light Your Fire

"THERE BE THREE things which are too wonderful for me, yea, four which I know not," said the wise man, "the way of an eagle in the air; the way of a serpent upon a rock; the way of a ship in the midst of the sea; and the way of a man with a maid" (Proverbs 30:18-19).

Well, there are five things that are too wonderful for me, yea ten, that light my fire. I share them here in the hope that your own imagination will be stirred to conjure up some goodies of your own.

A good meal in good company. The Bible says that in heaven folks will come from the east and the west and from the north and the south and sit at table in the kingdom of God. A foretaste of that goodly prospect is often experienced here and now when good friends gather to put their feet under the same table for good food and good fellowship. An unhurried prayer of gratitude to God, a cup of hot homemade soup, fresh corn bread cooked in an iron skillet and right out of the oven, real butter, savory roast, brown gravy, fresh corn on the cob, sweet potato souffle, fresh shelled black eyed peas, and hot coconut pie. I don't ask for much. Just a plain and ordinary little meal. Keep it simple. Take plenty of time. Drink a couple of glasses of really cold iced tea. And garnish the whole nine yards with good conversation. No wonder smart people want to go to heaven.

A walk in the woods. In the fall, you kick the leaves, revel in the color, savor the smells, walk a couple of fallen logs, sit on every stump you come to, marvel at the mushrooms, feast on a few dead-ripe persimmons sweetened to perfection for having hung for the last week or two in the wonderful warmth of the late fall sunlight, eat a bunch of possum grapes brought to their height of flavor by a couple of frosts, and at a little creek skip two or three flat rocks across the sun-dappled surface of still water. When you come to think of it, such a walk in the woods is worth a thousand dollars, maybe more.

A deep drink of cold water. When David was desperately weary, utterly exhausted, and sorely stressed by guerrilla warfare against the Philistines whose garrison was in Bethlehem where he grew up, he longed for "a drink of water of the well of Bethlehem which is by the gate." It's remembered from a far safer and more tranquil period in his life. He did not crave food. He did not ask for deliverance from his enemies. He did not ask for a nice bed with clean sheets—he longed for a drink of water. When a body is thirsty; nothing can compare with a drink of water.

Work. Does this seem odd to you? Probably not. When we stop to think about it, work is a very special gift from God. Work gives purpose to life. Work enables us to be useful and to feel that usefulness in our bones. When work is well done, it builds self-confidence. Work identifies us with God who is himself a worker. Work is the mother of sound sleep. Like others who write a little, I hate to write, but I like to have written. That is, the goads of discipline are for the moment grievous, painful, but there are special rewards once the work has been endured. So, thank God for work.

Butting heads with little grandkids. Some peculiar people, oddly enough, do not seem to relish this splendid sport. Gently butting heads with a three-year old little girl or a five-year old boy does for me, however, what it apparently does for a cow who nuzzles her calf and thus communicates affection, secures bonding, and shares by this unique sense of touch deeper feelings of love and pleasure and kinship than could ever be done with elemental sounds or mere words, no matter how intricately crafted or elegantly uttered.

Watching the sun set. Beautiful sunsets never, ever get boring. Lasting hardly longer than five or ten minutes, fine sunsets are infinitely varied, gloriously hued, wonderfully new, and breathtakingly original.

Seeing the moon rise. Few things in nature, or in all human experience, can rival a full moon inching up over the horizon on a late fall evening. It is a fascinating slow-motion marvel. As the earth does its inexorable turning, the faintest sliver of a big, golden moon peeps out, and then pushes up ever so deliberately until the whole gorgeous orb looks the world right in the eye. If you could only see this marvel once in a lifetime and could know what sheer delight it would be, you would gladly go halfway around the world to experience it. But for us, right where we live, it comes every 28 days. Enjoy.

Nestling down in a good bed for a night's sleep. And just to think. When I was a kid, I hated to go to bed at night lest I miss something exciting that might happen or something wonderful that could develop. Well, things have changed. Now I can hardly wait to get to that blessed bed. This is something that is nothing short of delicious: to get in a pleasantly warm bed on a cold, dark night, pull the covers up under my chins and then around my oversized ears, nestle down in the bed after a small spell of twisting and squirming so as to get fixed just right and then to listen to the little mountain stream making exactly the same gurgling, audacious music it did when I built that little cabin forty years ago—the same sound it was likely making 10,000 years before that. Do please excuse me. I can't stay awake any longer. Let's talk about it in the morning.

Staring at the fire. This has to be one of the oldest, simplest, and finest of all human pleasures. We're talking *neutral.* All gears are disengaged. All muscles are hanging loose. All electrical systems are unplugged. Tranquillity reigns. The flickering firelight makes its infinitely varied display but the real show is the coals. Some are red. Some are yellow. Some are white. Sooner or later they all get gray around their temples (don't we all?) as the ashes start to form. Gravity pulls the larger pieces down into a natural little heap, not totally unlike what is slowly transpiring on the surface of the sun where a somewhat different kind of fuel is being spent on its way to some far-off black hole. The visual wonders related to staring at a fire are enhanced, of course, by the welcome warmth that radiates a body's reveries. Anyone who cannot frequently sit in a rocker and stare at the fire is infinitely poorer for this deprivation. And all who share the blessing of this ritual are together in a select company of God's truly fortunate people.

Talk. Jean Paul Sartre allowed that the Frenchmen of his day were interested in only two things: to fornicate and to read the newspaper. Our baby boomers do not seem to be very interested in reading the newspaper. The Generation X people seem caught up in their version of going there and doing that. (Having already been there and done that, I could ask them some helpful questions if they were only interested.) And it strikes me that Generation Y (Youth) people have an absolute compulsion to move around and spend money, as long as they don't have to make it. Me. I'm from another generation, another era, maybe another planet. I like to talk. I relish talk. I crave talk. I revel in talk. I go out of my way to get involved in talk. Like the Australian aborigines who learn three or four utterly disparate languages in order to talk more and tell more stories, I admire those gifted persons who talk much and who talk well. A talk fest with a very small company of good friends with nobody trying to pull rank, nobody seeking to dominate, and nobody compelled to preen, is about as close to a "lovely" evening as I can conjure up.

So, here are ten things that are "too wonderful for me." If they didn't light my fire, I would just have to tell you *my* wood would be wet.

The Signed Blank Check

IT WAS MORE than 53 years ago. I had just turned 21. A never-to-be-forgotten summer had come to an end. Clarence Jordan had invited me to spend the time between Baptist Student Week at Ridgecrest and the beginning of graduate school at Southwestern Baptist Theological Seminary with him and his family at Koinonia Farm out from Americus, Georgia. I had jumped at the chance. The then brand new enterprise was just in its earliest stages. Clarence's idealism was contagious. His courage was awesome. His Christian scholarship was impeccable. His impact for Christ was emphatically growing.

We had a glorious summer. Clarence and I built a room for me to sleep in, in a corner of the downstairs part of his family's garage apartment. He and I poured concrete for the floor. (It has since been broken up I am told by some young whippersnappers from the Baptist Student Union at Wake Forest University.) We went all over that part of the country preaching and teaching and making melody. You could hardly be expected to understand the meaning of the Psalmist's "joyful noise" unless you could have heard Clarence and me with our musical instruments, him with his trumpet and me with my saxophone, rendering all the verses of "When I Shall Read My Title Clear to Mansions in the Sky" to the startled ears of those hapless Georgia Baptists who came in from their farms to those summer meetings.

We worked in the peanut patches. We cut some wood. We gathered wild grapes. We visited with the neighbors. We made ice cream. We studied the Greek New Testament. We took an occasional sashay into town. We worked at improving race relations. We had some kind of a wonderful, rip-roaring, rousing, delightful time.

The summer's end came all too quickly; and I got ready to head out for seminary. There was no money, of course. I figured on finding a church to be pastor of when school started back in Texas. Travel was no problem then for hitchhiking was a quite acceptable way to get from one place to another. As I started to go, Clarence pressed into my hand a piece of paper. It was a blank check, good for every penny Koinonia Farm had in the bank, made out to me and signed, "C.L. Jordan."

I never cashed the check, of course. I've still got it. It is a tangible reminder of Clarence Jordan's trust, of his encouragement, of his indomitable vision, of his fathomless faith, of his contagious Christian experience, and of his profound commitment to be a doer of the word.

I think Clarence Jordan was the finest Christian I have ever known. Many factors contribute to my feelings about that: his spell-binding teaching of the Sermon on the Mount, his riding of a motorcycle from Americus to Houston to speak at our Baptist Student Unions' fall retreat for the colleges of Houston, his fantastic Cotton Patch translations of New Testament writings, his prophetic zeal, his compassionate spirit, his Jesus-like generosity, his gentleness, and, of course, his signed blank check.

The lessons of a lifetime are wrapped up in this signed blank check which I'm holding in my left hand as I write this with my right hand. At the risk of being maudlin, I mention a few.

Faith is victorious even if it is dynamited.

Courage is contagious even if cowardice is endemic.

Compassion is communicable even if it gets turned out of the church or crucified.

Friendship is forever even after the grass grows over the red clay mound.

Giving is better than getting even if the check had been cashed.

Diatribe
on Cybernetics

THE HOTTEST PLACES in the Hereafter, it has occurred to me, may be reserved for the purveyors and promulgators of the cybernetic revolution.

I condemn it, of course, because I don't dig it.

Its mechanical mysteries frustrate me.

Its electrical complexities confound me.

Its charm eludes me.

Its devotees antagonize me.

Its evangelists drive me away before the invitation.

And its vocabulary paralyzes me: hard drive, floppy disks, bytes, megabytes, gigabytes, dot com, dot org, web page, download, software, on line, chat room. All this and more—much, much more, *ad infinitum.*

Like the Roman Catholic Inquisitors of Florence who put Galileo on trial, and then under house arrest for the rest of his life, for advocating a view the Pope held to be "absurd and false philosophically, because it is expressly contrary to Holy Scripture;" like English Luddites who wrecked all the newfangled weaving machines they could swing a sledge hammer at; like the Amish with their horses and buggies; like a smart but appropriately credulous old relative who never to his dying day for one minute believed that we ever put any man on the moon, I choose to withdraw as discreetly as possible from this cyberspace business.

It is a bad dream.

Maybe it will all just go away.

Computerites are from Mars.

Even typewriters were a misbegotten step in the wrong direction, starting us down a slippery slope from which we have found no way of turning back.

If a body is under some compunction to write, he needs a legal sized pad and a fountain pen.

If God had wanted us to peck out email messages on a computer, why would he ever have given us stationery, postage, and mail boxes?

Now tell me the honest truth.

Could you ever again have any respect for a grown man who would look in a tiny window of a miniaturized machine that flashed up orders which he would then, like a robot, mindlessly obey? Of course not! To take orders from such a glorified adding machine is altogether unseemly, not totally unlike bowing down before a wooden god which we might whittle out of a piece of lumber cut from of our own woodpile and then place reverently between two candles on the mantel in the living room.

Dumb city.

Like happy-clappy church services, SUVs, broccoli, rap music, boom boxes, television sets left on all the time, cold houses, barking dogs, indoor cats, line crashers, call waiting, and telephone marketing, the computer is just going to have to get along as best it can without me or my blessing. I have made up my mind.

Oh, if I were fifty years younger, it likely would be a different story. But that is a condition contrary to fact. So I plan to continue to trudge along in my familiar rut, not at all perturbed that a dreadful virus has just been reported to scare the living daylights out of my with-it friends who have all likewise with one accord bowed their knees to this baneful Baal. I wish them no ill. In fact, if the word had not been so pitifully and painfully politicized in recent times, I would say that I feel some authentic compassion for them.

Why this diatribe about cybernetics?

There are those who might say, "He has gotten crotchety in his old age." But the truth is that I have always been crotchety.

Others might think, "The complexities of this transistor-driven revolution have simply pushed him over the edge." But actually my mind seems to be about as clear as it ever was, which of course is not a very compelling observation.

Still others could analyze my mind-set on this matter thus, "Surely he has assumed this know-nothing stance out of some deep-seated inferiority complex." But if this is so, I don't feel it in my bones.

Yet another explanation might be put forward, "He is a Baptist." But my quintessentially Baptist disposition, while arguably predisposing me to certain contrarian leanings can hardly be blamed for my profound abhorrence of cybernetics for, after all, there are lots of my fellow-Baptists, just as principled as I am, or more so, who do not share my mind-set about this genre.

What then makes this tic tick?

In a word, I'm 77.

And besides, just because I'm not paranoid is no sign they're not really after me.

Of course, to show you that I am not totally intransigent and hopelessly out of touch but in fact am a congenial and quite sweetly reasonable chap, I have written this little squib about transistors:

Ode to a Transistor

> Little devil, little god,
> Miniscule and passing odd--
> Key to mankind's gnawing needs,
> Tool of earth's outreaching creeds--
> Hope of hungry, light for poor,
> Upthrown window, open door--
> Tiny instrument of hate,
> Love's wide-open, brand-new gate--
> Machination for man's greed,
> Shining prospect for his need--
> Countdown for the human race,
> Hotline to the world's last place--
> Through your compressed little pad
> Runs man's fate for good or bad.

And you must know that I did actually buy a cell phone some three months ago. I've already learned to turn it on and off. The dialing bit, however, is coming along very slowly and with great anguish.

Who knows? If I can't beat 'em, I might some day just join 'em.

No less an eminence than Ralph Waldo Emerson has noted that "a foolish consistency is the hobgoblin of little minds."

So, please stay tuned. I'm putting all of this under advisement.

Sunsets

THE SUNSETS WERE spectacular in East Texas where I lived as a boy. The house in which I was born and where I lived until I went away to college was happily situated, particularly so if a body had an interest in watching sunsets.

The lay of the land was just right. The place was on a gentle hill. There was a good-sized draw to the west. Beyond the draw there was a big, open field. Beyond the field was a clearing. The clearing then stretched westward for about a thousand miles. Hardly a tree to mar the view, as the saying went. The sun was at liberty to do its thing in the shank of the evening. About a hundred miles due west, the then smallish cities of Dallas and Fort Worth were producing just enough pollution in the vast western skies to aid and abet the evening sun in a profligate paintbrushing of the heavens.

There were towering thunderheads, wispy mares' tails, buttermilk skies, occasionally heavy cloud banks that hugged the horizon, and a kaleidoscopic combination of all of these. The colors were pink, purple, lavender, orange, gold, yellow, and red. Mostly red.

The sunsets were glorious. Incredible. Fantastic. Breathtaking. Beautiful. Lovely.

In our family of four, any member, either my mother or my daddy or my older brother or I, felt complete freedom, if not moral compunction, to call everybody else to come out and watch the sunset. We did it often. There was something restorational, healing, curative, blessed about standing there still and quiet for a while in the blazing color of those wonderful sunsets.

The experience brought a moment of magic to some pretty tough times. It drew our family together. It bonded my brother and me with the glue of geography and place and time that could be the stickiest stuff in the world. It overshadowed the economic depression and made us forget for a little while that the car had to be sold, that cotton was going in town for 50 dollars a 500-pound bale, that there was no money for garden seed, that there would be no new bicycles, that the mortgage payment on the farm inexorably was coming due, that Herbert Hoover was President, and that the quintessential Fundamentalist Frank Norris was charging regularly in his paper, which we took, that George Truett was a Modernist.

After what is now well over half a century, I remember the sunsets. I think of them a good deal more clearly and a great deal more happily than I do of the hard times.

In our present situation characterized by Paul's "fears within and fightings without," I propose to be still and know that there is God. I propose to remember who I am and whose I am. I propose to remember my calling from God in Christ Jesus. I propose to relish the challenge of change. I propose to work for "the night is coming." I propose to experience the bonding of geography and a place and time with my own kind of folks. I propose to remember that a man's life consists not in the abundance of the things that he possesses. I propose to think on those things that are lovely.

And I propose to watch the sunsets. I hear tell that once a day God still fixes one of them up for his kind of folks who are out there and looking.

On Being
Seventy Five

TODAY I AM seventy five. Exactly half way between the Bible's vaunted "three score years and ten" and the "four score" years which "by reason of strength" get meted out to a few.

It is a milestone calculated to invoke mellowness, if a body could only keep from nodding off.

Old Omar Khayyam hit the nail on the head: "The Bird of Time has but a little way to flutter—and the Bird is on the Wing." I have to tell you, I can feel it in my bones. Somewhat. Yes.

The wise old man of Ecclesiastes had himself been there and done that. Else he could hardly have understood the situation well enough to chronicle so insightfully the vivid realities of these yellow leaf years.

Years when, as he says, "the sun grows dark, and the light goes from moon and stars." (Cataracts? Glaucoma? One garrulous eye specialist who headed his department at the University Medical School where I had gone to get the very best analysis available, chattering to a half dozen eager young medical interns standing by as he peered into the inner recesses of my poor eyeballs through grossly dilated pupils gave this casual diagnosis: "Senile macular degeneration. Yuck." Hardly a bedside manner likely to guarantee those young whelps an early retirement from the practice of medicine as caring eye specialists.)

Years when "ladies at the lattice lose their lustre." (Must

we wallow in specificity? Could the media drag out the details for months or years?)

Years when "the sound of the mill runs low, when the twitter of birds is faint." (For me the loss of hearing has crept up on padded cat's feet so that everybody mumbles, nobody enunciates, and I couldn't understand one single word of what our granddaughter just said.)

Years "when old age fears a height." (Old bones heal slowly, so be careful out there and don't fall.)

Years when "even a walk has its terrors." (Dragons and demons may be lurking and who know what bankruptcies or black holes might engulf you?)

Years when the "hair is almond white, and he drags his limbs along as the spirit flags and fades." (Arthritis? Ministrokes? Altzheimer's?)

Until in due time we go to our "long, long home and mourners pass along the street, on the day when the silver cord is snapped and the golden lamp drops broken" (Ecclesiastes 12:1-8 Moffatt.) [Do read this whole fantastic passage in James Moffatt's hauntingly beautiful translation.]

I mention these matters not to wallow in morbidity or because I relish this cataloguing of the infirmities of old age. On the contrary, I came here to celebrate.

Here goes.

I'm here. Lots of folks I've known aren't.

I'm alive. Lots of old friends aren't.

I'm still happily married to Mary Louise to whom after 51 years I still sign all correspondence, notes, cards, complaints, and kudos, no matter how trivial or inconsequential, with Greek words which freely translated mean, "My life, I love you," and with whom we have together been blessed with three wonderful daughters, fine sons-in-law, and splendid grandchildren not a few.

I remember good parents and a good home. Many are not so fortunate to have such good remembers.

I remember good teachers. How blessed I was, and how blessed I am to this good day because of them.

I remember church. Some good and some not so good. But for me, far more good than bad.

And I remember friends. Without them life would have been thin and poor. And without them life today would be immeasurably thinner, infinitely poorer.

A fine passage in Anton Chekov's *The Cherry Orchard* catches Yermolay Alexeyevitch, a new-rich business man who has just come from the auction in the city where he has bought for 90 thousand rubles the ancestral home of the bankrupt aristocrat, Madame Lyubov Andreyevna.

> The cherry orchard's mine!...If my father and grandfather could rise from their graves and see all that has happened! How their Yermolay, ignorant, beaten Yermolay, who used to run about barefoot in winter, how that Yermolay has bought the finest estate in the world. I have bought the estate where my father and grandfather were slaves, where they were not even admitted into the kitchen....Music! Play up!

So, today, as the happy owner of memories more precious by far than "the finest estate in the world," I have invited you in, where the music is, to join me in remembering, in celebrating, and in giving thanks to God for his immeasurable grace.

Many happy returns of the day.

Of She Bears
and Y2K

VIRGIL SAID HE wrote poetry like a she bear, gradually licking the new born cub into shape. (It took him seven years to write the 2183 lines of the four *Georgics*.)

I am a little bit like Virgil. Make that a little bitty bit.

This offering has only very slowly been licked into some semblance of shape. For five years, I have usually tried to sound in these essays a light and, I have hoped, a sometimes lilting note. Under the general rubric of Paul's "...whatsoever things are...lovely...think on these things," I have aspired to elicit an occasional smile, spread a random ray of sunshine, accentuate the positive, and avoid making sows' ears out of silk purses.

At this moment, however, I feel under some constraint to be more sober.

The reasons:

(1)   This journal has now been published for five years, and this last issue of Volume 5 is something of a natural milestone ("curst be he," to borrow words from Shakespeare's modest tombstone in Stratford, who reads this as millstone);

(2)   In a few days now we are scheduled to close out one millennium and usher in a new one, a portentous occasion, as mortals reckon such things (I think it is to my credit that in five years I have never once in this column uttered the Y2K mantra); and

(3) Besides, at 76 I am terminally (I use the word, shall I say, macabrely) aware that I have not the leisure of eternity in which to prophesy for "the moving finger writes and having writ moves on" as old Khayyam put it. In the great Indianapolis 500 race of life the flags are long since down and the last laps have begun.

So, is there any word from the Lord?

One respected body of Christian believers, the Shorter Catechism Presbyterians, allows that the "chief end of man is to glorify God and enjoy him forever."

Unaccustomed as I am to doing everything "decently and in order," as those Presbyterians so admirably do, I am more inclined to pick at that morsel of truth than I am to swallow it whole; but, still it keeps rearing its handsome head to be the catalyst for this particular licking into shape of this particular cub.

What is to be said about this God we would glorify and enjoy forever?

God is. It is a faith declaration. As Job said, "I know that my Redeemer liveth" (19:25). In the late 1930s when Adolph Hitler was tightening his death grip on Germany, Karl Barth was driven from his teaching post at the University in Bonn. Fleeing to his native Switzerland he enlisted as a private in the army where he remained until the war was over. At that time he returned to his teaching position in Bonn. Amid the noise of the cranes and caterpillars rebuilding from the bombed rubble, Karl Barth assembled his first class for his first lecture. His first words were, "Ich Glaube än Gott"—I believe in God. Those are the first words of the Apostles' Creed. And those must be my first words here, "I believe in God." They are words to carry us into the new millennium.

If we are to glorify God and enjoy him forever, we must "believe that he is and that he is a rewarder of them that diligently seek him" (Hebrews 11:6). Moreover we have to know something about him.

These things we believe we know.

God is One (Deuteronomy 6:4; Mark 12:29; 1 John 5:7). The people of God are totally immersed in this profoundest of convictions. It is the first of the commandments. It is the clearest and plainest of God's revelations: God is one. He is "all and in all" (Colossians 3:11), but he is not many. He is omnipresent, but he is not fragmented. God is one and his people are to be like him in singleness of heart and mind and vision with one Lord, one faith, and one baptism.

God is Holy (Leviticus 11:44; Psalm 99:9; 1 Peter 1:16). Holiness means whole, wholly other, exalted, worthy, sacred; but it also means morally pure, perfect in goodness, complete in righteousness, upright, clean, ethically uncompromised and uncompromising. As God is holy, so his people are ordered to be holy. A tall order. It is the labor of a lifetime as believers work out our salvation with fear and trembling.

God is Spirit (John 4:24). He is more than matter, above matter, under matter, beyond matter. That God is spirit does not mean that he is anti-matter but that he transcends matter. As God is spirit, so his people are to be spiritually oriented, not preoccupied with Pokemon trivia or all the other things of this world, laying not up for ourselves treasures on earth where moth and rust corrupt and where thieves break through and steal.

God is Peace (Judges 6:24 RSV). It would be shocking if the great God of peace who taught his people to say Shalom had not revealed himself precisely as he has done in Gideon's words recorded in Judges 6:24, "The Lord is peace." Because God is peace, his peacemaker people are to do "the things that make for peace."

God is Light (1 John 1:5). In him is no darkness at all. He is characterized as *shekinah* glory, consummate brilliance, shining purifier, revealing redeemer, kindly light, "the Father of lights" (James 1:17). In the very beginning, as it is recorded in Genesis 1:3, God said, "'Let there be light'; and there was light." Joseph Haydn, on hearing the first public performance of *The Creation,* leaped from his seat at the great choral refrain "and there was light" and cried out, "I didn't write that. God did." So, God's people as "children of light" (Ephesians 5:8) who are ordained to be "the light of the world" (Matthew 5:14) are to "walk in the light as he is in the light" (1 John 1:7).

God is Truth (1 John 5:6). Pilate's question to Paul, "What is truth?" might rightly have been posed as "Who is truth?" for we believe not only that truth is of God, but that indeed God is truth. To say that the truth makes us free is to say that God makes us free. Like our Lord, "full of grace and truth" (John 1:14), Christians are to gird our loins with truth (Ephesians 6:14) and "provide things honest in the sight of all" (Romans 12:17).

God is Love (1 John 4:8, 16). This formulation identifying God with the self-giving, compassionate, outreaching, tender mercy which we call love is a wonderful way to say who God is. And the other side of the coin of love is justice for justice is love at a distance. God's people are ordained to love him with all our whole hearts and our neighbors as ourselves (Matthew 22:34-40; Mark 12:28-34; Luke 10:25-28).

God is Word (John 1:1). Genesis starts with, "In the beginning God" and the Gospel of John opens with "In the beginning was the Word and the Word was with God and the Word was God." A word is reason and reality expressed in a language that folks can understand. What an astounding and beautiful insight with which to consummate this licking. And what a wonderful thought it is to carry with us through the Christmas season and into the new millennium.

As morning stars sing again together and as all the children of God shout for joy (Job 38:7) in his grace, I hope we can join our lives in glorifying God and in accelerating our everlasting vocation of enjoying him forever.

Hey. The bird is on the wing. Put your machine in fast forward. Now is the time. This is the day.

The Joy of Eating

A MOTLEY CREW of Positive Thinkers have taken it upon themselves to write books aplenty and articles more than aplenty about The Joy of Cooking, The Joy of Sex, The Joy of This, The Joy of That, and The Joy of Nearly Everything Else Under the Sun, just barely short of The Joy of Having a Root Canal.

Over the recent holidays, Thanksgiving, Christmas, and New Year's Day, however, the Joy of Eating has washed over my psyche time and again. Why not extol the virtues of this special joy ere the days come on, as the author of Ecclesiastes says, when "I shall have no pleasure in them" (12:1)?

Holiday feasts are really wonderful events. Why let the Blue Noses of this world play the grinch to steal the pleasure from this wonderful experience? I think, therefore, that I want to slip with you into a small season of reverie about the Joy of Eating.

Let me share with you some precious memories, memories that come readily to mind about marvelous meals that, pardon the expression, flesh out these thoughts about the joy of eating. I will limit myself to ten of them though I could as easily square the ten and present a hundred. But then you might accost me as a glutton. Just remember that our blessed Lord, for going to parties and feasts and eating out often with sinners and publicans, was dubbed by his detractors "a gluttonous man and a winebibber" (Matthew

11:19). Please permit me to note that I myself have never ever bibbed wine.

1. My childhood home was not one of food deprivation. On the contrary, my Mother was a splendid cook and my Father was a willing and eager co-dependent in the enterprise. The boys in the family also fell to with a vengeance, leaving no biscuit unbuttered, no hot cornbread unslathered, and no heaping platter of fresh pork ribs unattended. Gastronomically challenged we were not. Of all my Mother's masterpiece meals, this one stands out with special stars, asterisks, and trumpet flourishes: succulent roast pork with velvety brown gravy, corn fresh from the field, cut off the cob and then scraped and stewed a little, potatoes in a cream sauce that was to compose odes about, hot biscuits which were without any peradventure of a doubt the best in the county—no, make that country—and when baptized in that fabulous brown gravy inevitably called for more. There was always an offering of dessert, but my own favorite was nearly always two or three of those marvelous little biscuits buttered back and then consumed with ample helpings of the homemade fig preserves for which my mother regularly took the blue ribbon at the Van Zandt County annual fair. (The judges would have deserved to be horsewhipped and banished from the county for life if they had denied my Mother those blue ribbons for those glorious fig preserves.)

2. Another homemade dinner comes to mind. This one is my wife's doing and is one of my all-time favorites: baked turkey—tender, moist, and hot—giblet gravy, cornbread dressing, not dry, with plenty of onions and lots of sage, fresh cranberry sauce, a sweet potato soufflé about which to

become unabashedly lyrical, whole green beans wrapped in bacon and then broiled to crisp perfection, hot cornbread, and after that, hot, fresh coconut pie. Talk about the joy of eating!

3. To go a little farther afield, I invite you to consider Brennan's in New Orleans, although their Houston establishment is equally outstanding. Their fried oysters are simply the best on earth, with or without pearls. They will offer you a dab of potatoes and something akin to a salad, but the fried oysters are their *piece de resistance*. Then their Bananas Foster are required to leave a body in an ecstatic state of exquisite torpor as one arises with substantial effort and waddles out the door.

4. Still more distant geographically but quite near and dear to my heart, is the world-famous Peking Duck. When this incredibly tasty dish is served up with Chinese delicacies, there are few things better to eat in this whole wide world. As for the details of those side delicacies, suffice it to say

> All things wise and wonderful,
> All things great and small,
> All things bright and beautiful,
> The Chinese eat them all.

5. Once upon a time I was on a preaching mission pressing the cause of Christian Ethics over the length and breadth of the Hawaiian Islands (21 sermons in 21 days) when a preacher friend and his wife took my wife and me to the windward side of the Island of Kauai, found a cozy little shelter under a high bluff, hollowed out by high tides and occasional tsunamis, made a fine charcoal fire in his

hibachi, and cooked ample quantities of teriyaki steak which he had marinated overnight and then laid lovingly on the grill over those hot coals. I do not recall whether there were any accoutrements, but the memory of that teriyaki steak with plain bread will linger with me, through thick and thicker, to my dying day.

6. In the old days New York City offered nothing more memorably delicious than dinner on a night out at Mama Leone's. More money can easily be spent at the Twenty One Club or dozens of other places, but the food was simply never as marvelous as it was at Mama Leone's: fresh shrimp cocktail, half a dozen oysters on the half shell, broiled fresh fish, stuffed deviled crab, steaming new potatoes, and then a generous rasher of spumoni befruited and benutted as if there would be no tomorrow. The glitz and the bustle left something to be desired in the realm of the aesthetic; but the food was sheer, unalloyed joy.

7. One of the best eating places on earth was, is, and I hope ever shall be, the Stagecoach Inn at Salado, Texas. For more than fifty years I have contributed materially to keeping them in business. To begin with, you are served a cup of exquisite, scaldingly hot chicken broth and about a half bushel of very special hushpuppies, water cornbread delicacies rolled up in little bitty rolls about the size and length of your little finger and served crisp and brown and hot with real butter from genuine cows. Then comes tomato aspic garnished with a dash of mayonnaise and a generous sprinkling of capers. Then they bring a plate of freshly barbecued chicken slathered with homemade tomato-based sauce and accompanied by fried bananas and oven browned potato wedges. Cold iced tea and a slice of lemon chess pie

to top it all off are enough to make a dog break a logging chain to get loose and get to it.

8. For many decades the best seafood feast I ever found in all in the world could be relished at the San Jacinto Inn hard by the Battleship Texas some thirty miles outside of Houston. Hungry landlubbers would be inundated from a set menu with fresh shrimp, fresh oysters, steamed crab, fresh fried fish, stuffed deviled crab, hot hushpuppies, hot biscuits, and tomato preserves. Wow. Joy.

9. For decades the world's best roast beef has been served up at the Monocle on Capitol Hill in Washington, D.C. If you are fortunate you may get the end piece with an ample supply of au jus. You can then take a small salad and a small baked potato and simply inhale the whole thing with a goodly portion of hot sour dough bread. Small wonder that famous men and women cross all lines of party and class to patronize this place. It's not the location. It's not the ambience. It's not the clientele. It's the roast beef.

10. For the nearly three decades that I lived in Nashville, the best eating place in town was the Satsuma Tea Room. This was a downtown establishment which served only lunch, five days a week. Presided over by Miss Arlene Ziegler who was the owner, manager, buyer, meal planner, and sometime cook, the Satsuma had one special meal every year just before Christmas. The whole city oriented itself to this Happening from about 3 p.m. until the food ran out about 9 o'clock. The spread was fabulous: baked ham, roast turkey, boiled shrimp, spiced round, Swedish meat balls, fish, chicken, even a plump roast pig with an apple in its mouth, salads, aspics, delicious vegetables (cooked, not the

raw ones that yuppies pretend to like), salads, deviled eggs, turkey hash, sweet potatoes, boiled custard, all kinds of great desserts, and bottomless cups of steaming hot coffee. One entered into this incredible experience without having eaten a bite of lunch and then exited some two hours later with no earthly intention of *ever* eating again.

Time and space have fled. As the author of Hebrews says, "Time would fail me to tell" of fried chicken and chicken gravy and hot biscuits served up at the world-famous Loveless Motel and Restaurant near Nashville, mouth-watering barbecued brisket all over Texas, Regas' world-class restaurant with unfailingly delicious meals in Knoxville, Mrs. Dickey's fried pies, Mrs. Wenske's glorious coconut cakes, Mobile's Original Oyster House, Hong Kong's fabulous Peninsula Hotel's storied Sunday buffets, the Kahala Hilton's coconut pies, Chuck's hamburgers, Mrs. Margurette Price's chicken and dumplings, and the storied Mama's Fish House on the windward side of the island of Maui.

Suffice it to say that of all human joys, not the least of these is The Joy of Eating. Bon apetit.

In Celebration
of Fire

FIRE WAS THOUGHT by ancient Greeks to have been brought to earth by Prometheus who had lighted a torch at the sun's chariot. In Rome the Vestal Virgins tended the sacred fire kept perpetually burning on the altar of the goddess Vesta. Earlier and more primitive people give evidence of having employed and treasured fire. It is now accepted that no fireless tribe of humans has ever been found.

I have just survived a winter ice storm in which fire took on new charm, new image, and new wonder.

Due to an utterly uncharacteristic attack of foresight, I had used one pleasant fall day, months ago, to lay by me in store a full cord of seasoned wood. Well. The thing that actually triggered this alleged foresight was a little ad, semi-literate, in the newspaper offering a full cord of wood for the decidedly reasonable price of $75, with an extra charge of $30 if they delivered it and stacked it. If you don't know, then let me tell you something. That is a very un-New Millenniumish price. So I called and took the woman up on the offer. She said yes, they would deliver the wood the next day. The next day I waited expectantly until it was pitch dark when I reluctantly gave them up, with not a few pejorative thoughts about the promise breakers. After a few days, however, my pejoratives cooled, somewhat. I would have called somebody else, but all of their prices were much too high for my emphatically plebeian inclinations. So I called my original firewood mongerer, she of the broken promises, and inquired as to what had happened. It seems that a few days before when they had finally got the trailer loaded with the wood, it was dark and that since their old truck didn't have any lights, they couldn't see to make the delivery. Okay, I allowed. Could they deliver it tomorrow? Yes.

So they came the next afternoon, about six of them in the odometer-challenged old pickup, pulling a long, ramshackled trailer loaded down with my wood. As they stacked this wood, it was plain to see that this was no ordinary load of wood. Believe me. There was pecan, mulberry, mesquite, hickory, elm, hackberry, pine, a little oak, and—hold tight—a generous sprinkling of bois d'arc. A little of it was the requisite 24 inches long. But most of it varied, free range—as they say, between 10 inches and 30 inches in length. No matter. At least not much matter. The fire hardly knows the difference anyway.

So, as I was saying when you interrupted.

There was this ice storm.

Now picture this. Snow and ice cover the ground. A blue norther has blown in. Nothing more substantial than a barbed wire fence has hindered it on its blustery journey between here and the North Pole. As the man said to Admiral Byrd at the South Pole in a howling blizzard, "Man, I bet it's cold in Amarillo today."

And now picture this. A fine stack of this aforementioned wood has been laid in my fine stone fireplace in my very pleasant study. The kindling has cooperatively caught the proffered spark. In short order, the fire and the wood have enthusiastically embraced each other. In one of the world's most splendid wonders, it has become a roaring fire.

And me? I have backed up to this thing of beauty, this joy forever, this splendid fire. And I am toasting my backside in a glorious ritual as old as humanity, although I can personally vouch for only 76 years of this glorious serendipity. Delicious. Wonderful. Fantastic.

Only reluctantly do I turn myself, not unlike a marshmallow held on a long fork over the fire and rotated just before it swells and bursts into flame.

In due time the fire burns down. Coals are formed and tumble in on each other. The andirons and the grate are white hot. I draw up my easy chair and prop my feet up on the foot high hearth, in a position calculated to toast them just right without harming my shoe soles. It is pure ecstasy.

"Paradise enow," as old Omar Khayyam was wont to say.

Drop by some winter day and join me for a visit by the fire. Proud to have you. We can just sit a spell and stare at the fire.

Dayspring

CHRISTMAS IS A TIME for celebrating.

No wonder that when I was a kid we shot off firecrackers, lit Roman candles, waved sparklers, killed the fatted chicken, feasted on fruit cakes, and generally made merry.

Christmas is a time for happiness.

It is a time for gifts, for angels, for stars, for music, for joy, and for lights.

When Christmas comes, the winter solstice is already past. The days are getting longer already. In the natural order of things, day has begun to conquer night. Things are looking up.

The people of God have special reason to rejoice for "the dayspring from on high hath visited us" (Luke 1:78). Consider this profundity in its context.

When pregnant Mary went from Nazareth "into the hill country" to see her cousin Elisabeth, herself six months pregnant with John, there was at their meeting a spirited exchange of epiphanies. Elisabeth burst forth first "with a loud voice" glorifying God; and then Mary's very soul overflowed with what we have come to call her Magnificat, her inspired utterance of praise to the Lord. Then, after an unreasonably long visit of three months with her kinswoman Elisabeth, Mary finally went home. Then, Elisabeth had her baby, and her husband Zacharias, mute since the angel of God first broke all this good news to him, lifted his own voice and "prophsied":

Blessed be the Lord God of Israel; for he hath visited and redeemed his people,
And hath raised up an horn of salvation for us in the house of his servant David;
As he spake by the mouth of his holy prophets, which have been since the world began;
That we should be saved from our enemies, and from the hand of all that hate us;
To perform the mercy promised to our fathers, and to remember his holy covenant;
The oath which he sware to our father Abraham, that he would grant unto us, that we being delivered out of the hand of our enemies might serve him without fear,
In holiness and righteousness all the days of our life.
And thou, child, shalt be called the prophet of the Highest; for thou shalt go before the face of the Lord to prepare his ways;
To give knowledge of salvation unto his people by the remission of their sins,
Through the tender mercy of our God; whereby the dayspring from on high hath visited us,
To give light to them that sit in darkness, and in the shadow of death, to guide our feet into the way of peace.

The Oxford English Dictionary, the best in our language, says that dayspring means daybreak or early dawn. The word is now said to be chiefly poetic or figurative. It is generally designated as archaic. Our vocabularies are poorer; however, for our abandonment of this remarkable word, dayspring.

As Zacharias understood, dayspring speaks of Christmas, of the dawn of grace, of the light of the world, of unconquerable hope.

Dayspring's spirit is caught in Suzy Best's beloved Christmas poem:

That night when in Judean skies the mystic star
    dispensed its light
A blind man moved in his sleep and dreamed
    that he had sight.
That night when shepherds heard the song of
    hosts angelic choiring near
A deaf man stirred in slumber's spell and
    dreamed that he could hear.
That night when o'er the new born babe the
    tender Mary rose to lean
A loathesome leper smiled in sleep and dreamed
    that he was clean.
That night when to the mother's breast the little
    King was held secure
A harlot slept a happy sleep and dreamed that
    she was pure.
That night when in the manger lay the
    Sanctified who came to save
A man moved in the sleep of death and dreamed
    there was no grave.

And dayspring's spirit brings to mind the conversion to Christ of the authentically pious Blaise Pascal. Of this remarkable French scientist, philosopher, and mathematician, William L. Hendricks has written, "It would be overly dramatic, but not without a kernel of truth, to say that everyone who has had an injection, used a thermometer, ridden a bus, used an adding machine, or studied higher mathematics has been influenced by Blaise Pascal" who "was instrumental in the discovery or advancement which made possible all of the above." Like Saul's encounter with God on the Damascus road when "there shined round about him a light from heaven," Pascal's experience of meeting God was bathed in the ineffable light of what he perceived to be God's "FIRE." That experience of grace came in 1654. His account of it was written on a fragment of parchment found sewn into his clothing after his death. His enlightenment came, his note revealed, "from about half past ten in the evening until past midnight"; and issued in "certainty, certainty, heartfelt joy, peace…joy, joy, tears of joy…everlasting joy…."

Does not his experience capture something of the miracle of the new birth? Does it not communicate something of the wonder of God's grace? And does it not radiate something of the glorious light of our God whom James referred to as "the Father of lights?"

Our Creator-Redeemer whose *shekinah* glory, whose shining presence, incarnated, has come as the dawn to our dark world.

The Dayspring from on high has visited us.

Hallelujah.

Amen.

What's the Good Word?

A WORD FITLY SPOKEN is like apples of gold in baskets of silver.

The wise man who wrote this proverb understood that words can be priceless treasures. They can be sublimely beautiful, marvelously powerful, immeasurably effective.

When John introduced his Gospel by saying that "in the beginning was the Word, and the Word was with God, and the Word was God," he laid out one of the profoundest concepts ever to engage the human mind. Its profundity is fathomless and its simplicity is sublime.

Mark Twain is said to have observed that the difference between the right word and almost the right word is the difference between lightning and a lightning bug.

It was the search for exactly the right word and precisely the right combination of words that kept Virgil at the hard work of composing his masterpiece, *The Georgics*, for seven long years even though it consisted of only 2183 lines.

Charles Rann Kennedy says in *The Terrible Meek*, "all the things that ever get done in the world . . . are done by words."

Christendom's peerless theologian and the author of *The City of God*, Augustine, referred to himself as "a peddler of words."

Though the Temple of Solomon in Jerusalem, the Parthenon in Athens, and the Forum in Rome have long since fallen in ruins, their ideas live on because of their words.

A baby's first word is the occasion for any family's delight and celebration. After making marvelous little pre-speech sounds for weeks, the small creature one day forms an actual word, a sound that makes sense. Soon there is another word, and then another, until torrents of words tumble out in one of the most remarkable of all human achievements—human speech. In spite of many books and uncounted articles that have been written about the origin of human speech, there is much about the phenomenon that is still utterly unknown and that is quite possibly unknowable.

Words are a perfect wonder.

Gibberish, on the other hand, is nonsense. It is sound and fury signifying nothing. Without meaning it carries no message. It communicates no sense from the one mouthing it or to the one hearing it.

A word "fitly spoken," however, is reason expressed in a language that others can understand. It makes sense. It communicates. It carries meaning. It can be strangely powerful.

In coming now to say something about the Christmas word, it should be understood that this is rightly perceived to be a deeply sobering responsibility. Yet it has exhilarating potential. The matter needs not be obfuscated with much speaking but ought to be so simple and plain that "wayfaring men, though fools, shall not err therein" (Isaiah 35:8).

The Christmas word is *Immanuel*. God is with us. The eternal Word of God has become flesh. The Creator has identified with the creature. Divinity has embraced humanity.

The Christmas word is *Incarnation*; and incarnation is the best communication ever conceived by God or humankind.

The Christmas word is *Grace*; and God's amazing grace everlastingly trumps human inadequacies, human stumblings, human sin.

The Christmas word is *Joy*; joy to the world so that the pain of birth is totally eclipsed by the joy of new life.

The Christmas word is *Giving*; and we know deep down, at this season better than any other, that giving is better than getting, that it is God-like to give.

The Christmas word is that there is a *Star* in the sky; a Star shining bright even though there are ominous clouds on the horizon.

The Christmas word is that there is a *Song* in the air; and the Song's pure beauty overrides the noise of braying donkeys, bleating sheep, bawling cows, and all the cacophonies that this old world can dream up and hurl at us.

The Christmas word is *Angels*, messengers of God, innumerable angels over us and around us and among us although the cruel oppressor's ruthless legions are garrisoned ever so nearby. God's messengers are hardly subject to our human weights and measures. All our puny attempts to weigh them and measure them and get them to hold still while we corner them and count them remind me of my old theology professor W. T. Conner's dry witticism that "it's really better not to know so much than to know so much that's not so."

The Christmas word is *Good News*; and God's irrepressible Good News has come just as fully and freely to unwashed shepherds in the fields keeping watch over their flocks by night as to the rich in their fine, warm houses, or to the high and mighty in their ivory palaces.

The Christmas word is *Salvation*, the salvation word which God had determined to say before the foundations of the world were laid, salvation that is simple and not complex, practical and not theoretical, clear and not garbled, understandable and not incoherent, kind and not cruel, good and not evil.

The Christmas word is that the *Kingdom of God* has now come; the kingdom of right relationships which was coming, has come, and now is.

So come and join in the Christmas parade.

Step lively to the beat of this Different Drummer.

Say *Yes* to all the promises and "yesses" of God that in the fullness of time have found their consummate Yes in Jesus Christ.

What's the good word? The good word is Merry Christmas.

And God bless us every one.

The Letter
Giveth Life

THE WORLD HAS Brother Paul to thank for the valuable saying that "the letter killeth, but the spirit giveth life" (2 Corinthians 3:6). How very true. The wisdom of the saying is crystal clear. We are not to get so bogged down in dotting the "I"s and crossing the "T"s that we lose the sense of what is intended. Especially in good old freedom-loving America we are inclined to such a rejection of rules and standards, to such a bias against instructions and guides, and to such negativism about directions and "How To" counsels, however, that we are now edging perilously near to a general lawlessness that is closer to anarchy than it is to civilization.

I am remembering that two of my friends were flying one day to a meeting that I had called. One of the friends, John Claypool was much inclined to deep thoughtfulness bordering on authentic profundity. He turned to his traveling companion in the seat next to him, Henlee H. Barnette, and asked, "Henlee, isn't every issue in life characterized by ambiguity?" John told me later that Henlee looked out the window in silence a long time and then turned to him to say, "Yes and No."

We are agreed, I trust, that "the letter killeth but the spirit giveth life." Please ponder, however, the possibility of truth in this proverb's mirror image. Consider, "The spirit killeth but the letter giveth life."

Please don't fly off in a fit of rage, withdraw fellowship

from me, or write me out of your will. At least, not just yet. Maybe later.

When asked whether or not Pentecostals would get to heaven, my old theology professor, Dr. W.T. Conner, at seminary replied, "Why, yes, of course—if they don't run right past it." He was a wise man and not given to disparaging remarks about the religion of others. He was simply reflecting a rather commonly held opinion in those heady days of Pentecostalism's early zeal that "spirit" sometimes seemed to eclipse "letter" in their wonderful enthusiasm.

If we have an overdose of "spirit" and an underdose of "letter," then we tend toward such self-centeredness, lack of discipline, and even lawlessness that our energies and life itself can be poured out like water. In truth, we need buckets in which to hold the water. We need fences to keep us in the pasture. We need rules that will give us some sort of ordered environment. We need governance to keep every person from simply doing that which is right in his own eyes to his own detriment and to the possible harm of those about him. We need the letter of the law, lest following what is subjectively thought at the moment to be the spirit of the law each person sets his own boundaries, acts on his own whims, and is motivated solely by feelings so that nothing is agreed on that is for the common good. With such a scenario, civilization would vanish in a fog of egotistical formulations guaranteeing that we would not learn from those who have gone before us.

Anarchy can never be as appropriate for humanity as the order which is characterized by boundaries, fences, walls, and rules.

In this light, then, too much "spirit killeth" but the letter "giveth life."

In our Western culture, musicians accept a contrived scale within which they function professionally. The *Encyclopedia Britannica* says, "Hence diatonic music gives a general impression of strength, simplicity, and solidity as distinguished from the more restless and poignant character of that in which notes from foreign keys are introduced by accidentals." Without the agreed on boundaries, music as we know it would not be possible. The "letter" of the boundaries "giveth life" to the music we love.

Those libertines who seek to live outside the laws of society and of God, unrestrained by convention or morality, consistently dash their life vessels against the rocky breakers of dissolution and ruin. Acceptance of the laws of God and the disciplines of society could save them from this folly.

In the Christian social ethics garden in which I have, to use the somewhat inelegant phrase from the King James Version of the gospels, "digged and dunged," a lot of passers-by have sniffed that specific attention to the "letter" of Christian social ethics is beneath them. They choose to pass by on the other side, think deep thoughts, philosophize about profound principles, write weighty position papers to be read by their peers, and to publish ponderous tomes.

In the meantime, average students and ordinary church members smoke cigarettes and get lung cancer, drive carelessly and kill themselves, drink alcohol and become addicts, take a little marijuana and then become hooked on cocaine, play it cool with a little gambling and slip into pathological compulsiveness in an immoral effort to get something for nothing, toy with pornography and trash the possibility of a happy marriage, and dabble with a little adultery but then slide painfully into abortion.

For heaven's sake.

Get real.

The "spirit giveth life" and light on all these things to be sure.

But plain, practical, specific, unambiguous, unvarnished talk, teaching, preaching, and action are needed if the slippery slope to ruin is to be avoided. Multitudes will miss the message unless it can be remembered that too much of the spirit killeth, but the letter giveth light.

❡ Ten Good Things ❡

FOR MANY YEARS the editors of *USA Today* asked me to write a column for their first issue of the New Year. Their assigned topic was "Ten Good Things that Happened" during the past year. It was a pleasant exercise. Without meaning to appropriate the idea for this present occasion, I sat down recently and reviewed the year 2000 to see what might pop into my head. Sure enough Ten Good Things came to mind.

Would you be willing for me to share them with you?

Life and a measure of health were extended to me. The ongoing gift of life itself could never be basely taken for granted. On the contrary, life last year seemed to me to be more and more the special gift of God; and I have savored it day-by-day, week-by-week, and month-by-month. Moreover, God forbid that I should consider the measure of health which I have experienced as anything but undeserved, unearned, and unmerited icing for the cake of life. In the year 2000, God did this again for me and for most of those I truly love. I am much obliged.

Family and a measure of joy were embraced. The richest blessings of life were encompassed in this circle of family. Godly parents, a wonderful wife of 53 years at this writing, three splendid daughters, fine sons-in-law, five marvelous grandchildren, brothers who are both kin and kindred spirits, and a cloud of cousins near and far, close and distant, have affirmed us, propped us up in our leaning places, and furnished us a context for joyous and abundant living. Things could not even begin to be as good without them.

Friendships and a measure of Enrichment were experienced. Let me illustrate with how we have capsuled in a two-day get-together on Valentine's Day an institutionalized Friendship Festival. Friends from near and far come flying in, driving in, shuffling in, and hobbling in. Some spend the night with us, staying up late and talking non-stop. Some get up early. Some sleep late. All eat a right smart. We have a big Luncheon Blowout at Neiman Marcus' Iris Room where they clear off a wide space for us and try to stay out of our way. We share news, tell yarns, make jokes, and do what we can to keep one another appropriately humble. Nobody has an agenda. We are totally and happily relaxed. As one of them e-mailed back the next day after returning to his home, "It just doesn't get any better than that." So. It really doesn't.

Peace and a measure of justice were proffered and, in various ways, accepted. There is a biblical figure of speech which speaks of righteousness and peace kissing each other (Psalm 85:10). When righteousness, or justice, come out on top of all our strivings, peace prevails. This is not just an absence of hostility but a shalom of heavenly proportions, a peace that has surmounted injustice, soared above strife, and broken down middle walls of partition. Some great points of light during the past year have been the incredible work of many who have done the things that make for peace. We gratefully salute them.

Deliverance and a measure of closure for some of the loads
I had shouldered were tendered and thankfully received. A
Director, Dr. Robert Kruschwitz, was enlisted and installed
for the Center for Christian Ethics at Baylor University, the
consummation of a decade of prayers, hopes, and dreams.
An Editor, Dr. Joe Trull, took the torch for publishing
Christian Ethics Today and with the enlistment of a new
Board of Directors has successfully completed the sixth
year of this journal's publication. My own sense of
deliverance from these duties has been capped with a
deeply satisfying sense of closure regarding my own part in
these enterprises. They are in good hands, and I
wholeheartedly bless them.

Work and a measure of fulfillment continued. I never
doubted that they would. Fate handed me a lemon in the
form of the Great Depression when I was six years old. That
long night began in 1929. Hard Times. But my family, with
the help of God, made what little lemonade we could of it.
I went to work. And I have been working ever since. Like
Virgil's Aeneas who kept bending his personal will to that
of his divine mandate to found and build the city of Rome,
I have not been disobedient to my own heavenly vision. I
have stayed hitched, continuing to heed what I have
perceived to be the high calling of God in Christ Jesus to
help "changed people change the world." God has set before
me a bountiful table of marvelous fulfillment. There are
signs, moreover, that he may not be plumb finished.

Ordering and a measure of alignment began to fall into place
during the year 2000 in ways that made life better and more
satisfying. Too much work can be as hurtful as too little
work. For most of my life, for whatever neuroses may have

been goading me. I've worked too hard, burned the candle at both ends too foolishly, and undertaken too much. Now at long last I am beginning to find breathing room, gradually getting my house in order, and slowly catching up on lots of things too long pushed aside. There is an insightful and moving old pioneer gospel song that speaks of the world's turning and turning till it turns around right. Right on. It's a good feeling to see things turning around right, to be getting some of my ducks in a row.

Calm and a measure of assurance. When the Bible says that the stars in their courses fought against Sisera, the Canaanite enemy of the people of God, it is a way of saying that this is a moral universe. Ultimately all those who array themselves against the redemptive and just purposes of the Lord God are destined for defeat. Conversely, those who identify themselves with God and his righteous rule can relax in calm assurance. Some propitious developments came together last year to blanket me with a sort of cosmic calm bringing reassurance that God's people are everlastingly covered with God's gracious hand. This is insurance guaranteed not to lapse.

Providence and a measure of rest. Providence can be a kind of synonym for Deity; and it can also be a noun that speaks of care, foresight, and advance planning. It has seemed to me that the past year has brought abundant evidence of God's providence, care when it is needed most. Things have been clearly seen as having worked together for some good to those who love the Lord and are called according to his purpose (Romans 8:28). When the profundity of this truth is embraced, there comes deep rest, deliverance from weariness, despair, commotion, annoyance, confusion, and agitation. Such tranquility has often been the wonderful gift of God throughout the past year, a foretaste of the blessing of rest in eternity which God is preparing for those who love him.

Grace and a measure of blessing were bestowed beyond what might have been asked or thought. What more could be said? Praise God from whom all blessings flow.

Now, lest I leave you with the impression that I am hopelessly Pollyannaish, I offer a caveat. Yes, I know about sin, evil, failure, pain, suffering, injustice, and death. Yes, I am aware of a personal diminution of strength, some fading of vision (the medical texts call it by the decidedly inelegant name of senile macular degeneration), a gradual shutting down of the functions of my auditory nerves, and the steady demise of millions of brain cells. Yes, like T. S. Eliot's J. Alfred Prufrock who saw the moment of his greatness flicker, who saw the Eternal Footman hold his coat and snicker so that, he says, "in short, I was afraid," so I lived last year with a rather vivid awareness of the frailty of my humanity. And that awareness, if anything, is increasing as life goes as on. And yet . . . .

Yet. Yet these ten good things remembered are not figments of the imagination. They are real. And so "if there be any virtue, and if there be any praise, think on these things" (Philippians 4:8).

Wisdom

THE GENRE WHICH I have generally used in writing for this journal has been one of intentional low voltage. (Admittedly, this has not been a strain for me for low voltage is one of my very best things, my *modus operandi*, as it were.) Other contributors have provided the meat of strong doctrine, while still others have addressed the weightier issues of Christian social ethics. I have tried to focus on such things as Paul, I imagine, must have envisioned when he wrote the wonderful insights of Philippians 4:8, "Whatsoever things are . . . lovely . . . think on these things."

In recent times, however, I have been so driven to wade more daringly into the deep waters of the concept of wisdom and so compelled to try to find ways to communicate the importance, if not the primacy, of wisdom that I simply cannot now be disobedient to what I have perceived to be this "heavenly vision." Woe to me if I preach not this gospel.

A few months ago my motor was turned over regarding this business at hand when an acquaintance from another state wrote to ask me to respond to some penetrating questions and stimulating ideas about wisdom. It seems that he was writing a doctoral dissertation about wisdom and wanted a little input from an elder (I've turned 78 now) on the subject.

I gave it careful thought, and have continued to do so

across several months. So, buckle up and hunker down. I'm fixing to make a run at wisdom.

Wisdom is a subject that deserves more attention than it has recently been given and obviously more than I can possibly give it here; but perhaps a quick look may prove to be better than no look at all.

Wisdom is that quality of personhood associated with good sense, gumption, judgment, discernment, knowledge, prudence, enlightenment, and insight. Wisdom distinguishes between good and bad and then between better and best. Wisdom tells the difference between right and wrong. Wisdom discerns the distinction between light and darkness, prudence and foolishness, aspirations and appetites, discipline and desire, timeless values and transient whims. Wisdom perceives the true and moves toward the true. Wisdom has to do with the exercise of sound judgment in choosing right means to attain right ends. Wisdom understands that you don't burn down a cathedral to fry an egg even if you have a ravenous appetite.

That wisdom is today in astoundingly short supply is not debatable. Its scarcity is evident in public life, in organized religion, in international doings, in economic affairs, in politics, and in family relationships.

The Bible teaches that the fear of the Lord is the beginning of wisdom (Psalm 111:10; Proverbs 9:10). The Bible's "wisdom literature"—Job, Proverbs, and Ecclesiastes—constitutes a major category in the Scriptures. And the New Testament's little book of James, the favorite book in the Bible for many, might well be called "The Wisdom of James" for as Martin Luther grudgingly admitted after having omitted it entirely from his first edition of his German translation of the Bible and then included it in the second edition, for he said, "It has many a good saying in it." The dour monk was wise to come around.

Who is wise?

By asking this question, some specificity may be realized which would otherwise elude us. I hope we can agree that a person is wise who has at least the following characteristics.

A wise person fears God and keeps his commandments. That is, a wise individual respects God, honors God, obeys God, and loves God. When asked by the lawyer which was the greatest commandment in the law, Jesus answered wisely with the great Hebrew Shema, "Hear, O Israel; the Lord our God is one Lord: And thou shalt love the Lord thy God with all thy heart, and with all thy soul, and with all thy mind, and with all thy strength: this is the first commandment, and the second is like, namely this, Thou shalt love thy neighbor as thyself" (Mark 12:29-31).

A wise person sees. That is, a wise individual is a consistent seer, a perceiver, a discerner, continually seeking knowledge, understanding, perception, and insight that will bring deliverance from pitfalls, the safety that comes from walking daily in the light, and a growing commitment to wholeness and holiness which leads more and more toward the perfection which our Lord has challenged his people to strive for. Did not Robert Browning glimpse this when he wrote, "Trust God, see all, nor be afraid"?

A wise person takes the long look. That is, a wise individual is not shortsighted, is not foolhardy, counts the cost before embarking on a new enterprise, and looks before leaping.

A wise person listens. That is, a wise individual asks, hears, welcomes counsel, learns from others, and stays teachable so as to profit from the lessons of history, the advice of those with experience, and the accumulated lessons learned by those who have gone before.

A wise person combines patience with enthusiasm. That is, the wise individual's life and work are characterized on the one hand by calmness and composure in the realization that sometimes it is required of us that we wait on the Lord and on the other hand that fervor, ardor, zeal, and passion are qualities without which not much good ever gets done.

A wise person does right consistently. That is, a wise individual understands that honesty is the best policy, that purity is better than filth, that love is better than hate, that giving is better than getting, that building is better than burning, that peace is better than war, and that it is better to suffer for righteousness' sake than to compromise with evil.

A wise person acts. That is, a wise individual, even while understanding the ambiguities of life and realizing that many difficult decisions are not subject to absolute black and white resolution, refuses to be everlastingly stalled in neutral, always immobilized, and forever dallying on the plains of hesitation, like T. S. Eliot's J. Alfred Prufrock descending the stairs in anguished consternation as he tries to decide whether or not he dare eat a peach. Wisdom requires action, work, involvement, and an incarnational commitment to be about the Father's business, actively working to redeem the time.

Too hurried to be still and know that the Lord is God,

too harried to possess our own souls, too busy to take even one day out of seven to rest, too preoccupied with pleasure to experience joy, too busy getting and spending on earth to lay up for ourselves treasures in heaven—modern people keep stumbling past the gate of wisdom.

There is a better way.

It is the way of intentionally seeking, and by God's grace, actually apprehending, wisdom.

More than almost all other virtues, wisdom is found by those who seek her. A good start in that search is to read carefully the book of Proverbs. Then read the book of James. Then find some wise old persons with whom to sit down and talk at length to discover what they have to teach you. Then read such literature from the classics as may appeal to you. Start anew in whatever way seems right to you, a renewed journey into the world of wisdom. In that world is peace that passes all understanding, riches more precious than silver or gold or stocks or bonds or houses or lands, and abundance of life beyond anything we might imagine to think or to ask.

"Wisdom," Jesus said, "is justified of her children" (Matthew 11:19).

Cars. Cars. Cars.

NO COUNTRY ON earth has had a more torrid love affair with cars than America.

My own infatuation with the genre, however, has been somewhat fickle.

In 1925 when I was two years old, my Daddy bought a brand new 1925 Model T Ford. He paid $439.69 for it according to the receipt which I still have, with the charges broken down: $355 for the "Ford Touring" car itself, $63.90 for freight, $17.40 for tax, and $3.39 for nine gallons of gas and six quarts of oil. This car was just a normal part of my early childhood until the Great Depression. We sold it in 1930 without fanfare when we could no longer buy gasoline for it. Don't cry for the Model T, Argentina. Life went on.

A few years later our family bought a 1935 Ford sedan, which I, as a teenager, neither wrecked nor killed myself in. It is best remembered for its simple utilitarian purposes: hauling tomatoes into town to the market, transporting our family to and from church services, and, with my older brother driving, carrying me and my small suitcase off to Baylor to start to college in 1940. I attach no stars or streamers, bells or whistles to it, although the car did have some saving graces, which ought not now to be denied or denigrated or basely forgotten.

In late 1944 I was called to be pastor of the Baptist church at Golden, some 120 miles from Fort Worth where I had launched into a five-year program of seminary studies.

Fate, and I suppose a bit of hard luck, brought into my life at this time a 1937 Dodge sedan, which used machine I employed to go back and forth between Fort Worth and that wonderful church field in East Texas. Here this plot begins to thicken.

W.F. Howard at that time was head of Baptist student work for Texas Baptists, and he wanted to put a youth revival team to work across the state so as to try to spread abroad some of the remarkable revival stirrings that had begun at Baylor in Waco. I was chosen as one of the two preachers for that first youth revival team of five. The aforementioned Dodge may well have been a factor in that choosing and definitely was a major player in that hot summer of 1945. The car was big, it had a large trunk, and it gave some promise of being able to waltz across Texas for eleven revivals in eleven weeks. So it did—from Galveston to Breckenridge, from Texarkana to Harlingen, and from Ennis to Sulphur Springs with five (5) people and all of our paraphernalia. The load was heavy, however, and the old car resisted the burden. It often overheated, hence its name, the Van Zandt CountyFireball.

But the saga proceeds and the plot further thickens.

I also used this old Dodge to shuttle back and forth from Fort Worth to Houston to see Mary Louise. I had proposed marriage to her on our second date, having postponed this momentous matter as long as I could have reasonably been expected to drag it out and wait around one bit longer. In spite of weekly drives from Fort Worth to Houston, it took her an agonizing two years to say "Yes." Hasty decisions have never been her long suit. But the old Dodge was, again, a major player in my successful courtship of this lovely young woman who became my wife.

In the fullness of time, the Van Zandt County Fireball,

bless its sainted memory, was traded in for a new 1947 Plymouth, for "to everything there is a season." In short order that car was traded in for a new Chevrolet. Then there was another trade for another new Chevrolet. Then quite soon there was a new Buick. In fact, I traded cars so fast and furiously in those halcyon days of my callow youth that my excesses put a not inconsiderable strain on the happy marriage that Mary Louise and I were beginning to negotiate. With four children and the help of Baptists firmly committed to keeping preachers poor if not humble, however, I came off that new car-buying binge. Cold turkey! By 2001, I had not bought a new car in 17 years. This latter day excessiveness, negatively calculated, once again put a not inconsiderable strain on the aforementioned happy marriage which by this time had endured for 54 years

One evening a couple of months ago in rather uncharacteristic huffiness, Mary Louise shared with good friends over an unfriendly game of Scrabble, "Foy is NEVER going to buy a new car." I had no earthly idea she cared. So I went out the next day and bought a new car. You can't imagine how cars have changed in the last 17 years: automatic transmissions, air conditioning, power windows, power seats, thermostats, CDs, variable speed windshield wipers, tinted glass, and other accoutrements remaining to be explained or even discovered.

But please don't go away yet. There is a *piece de resistance* yet to come. Along the way yet another car came into my life. And as Robert Frost said in the closing line of *The Road Not Taken*, "That has made all the difference."

The year was 1960. I had built a cabin in 1958 at 9500 feet altitude in a blue spruce valley about 20 feet from a rushing mountain stream at Red River, New Mexico. Now, honestly, I've never really been much for coveting things. I must confess, however, that I developed a downright prurient craving for some sort of old four-wheel drive vehicle that would be happy in that special Rocky Mountain environment.

My Red River friend, Mont Dalton, found one in a barn near his ranch in Chattanooga, Oklahoma. It was a 1946 Willys Jeep painted a bright turquoise over the original coat of army green, with fine yellow wheels. The owner was willing to part with it for $350. My friend shook hands with the owner and towed it 400 miles to Red River where I lovingly embraced it, pressed it to my bosom (it didn't have a top), and adopted it into my family as one of our very own natural-born children.

I built a small shed for it, put new tires on it (they are still on it, of course, for it has been only 41 years), became accustomed to its idiosyncrasies (such as turning on the ignition by pulling the switch labeled "Lights"), and proceeded to haul children and friends up and down old gold mining roads, through uncounted mountain streams, around hair-raising switch-backs, and through fantastic adventures which were more fun than Training Union and Deacons' Meetings put together.

From this old Jeep we have seen elk, bear, deer, bighorn sheep, badgers, coyotes, wolves, and once a big mountain lion slinking furtively across the trail right in front of us. We have seen choke cherries, wild raspberries, mountain strawberries, gooseberries, and blueberries. And we have driven up on patches of delicate irises, clumps of exquisite columbines, meadows full of deep purple gentians, brilliant purple asters, colonies of daisies in full bloom, fields of butter-and-eggs which any self-respecting florist would fight for, and breathtakingly beautiful mountainsides of great quaking aspens in their frost-blessed garments of solid gold.

When we offered to give the cabin to our youngest daughter on her fortieth birthday with all the rights and privileges and heartaches appertaining thereto, she readily accepted the gift on the condition that the Jeep go with it.

And so it did. It continues to start every year after having been left for the winter in temperature dropping to 40 degrees below zero, as it has for 41 years. A thing of beauty and a joy forever.

If you even start to think them not lovely, then pause for a little while and consider what life would be like without cars.

Cars. Cars. Cars. Long live cars.

Christmas:
Magic and Miracle

Christmas is a magic word.

It is laden with a thousand images.

Images bright and beautiful, warm and wonderful,
exciting and joyful.

Christmas, however, is more than magic.

It is miracle. It is God's doing.

Like a treasured gold coin, Christmas has two sides. One
is magic; the other is miracle. One is natural; the other is
supernatural. One is of the earth, earthy; the other is
straight from the heart of God, heavenly.

It is right for us to affirm both, to reject neither, to
embrace the whole.

Christmas, of course, means different things to different
people. Country people have a take on it that is different
from city people. Children understand it differently from
adults. Poor folks face it with different recollections and
different expectations than the rich. The Americans and
the English, in spite of our common language, experience
Christmas in quite different ways. Germans and Italians
have significantly different perceptions of the season.
Christmas celebrants in the Northern and Southern
Hemispheres naturally mark the occasion in strikingly
different ways. The dour Puritans rejected the holiday
altogether, seeing it as a popish practice with which true
believers should have no truck; but faithful Roman
Catholics were admonished by no less an authority than

Pope Gregory I in 601 A.D. to "celebrate a religious feast and worship God by their feasting, so that still keeping outward pleasures, they may more readily receive spiritual joys."

Only God in heaven now knows, of course, actually *when* Jesus was born. Various dates were vigorously debated for the first five hundred years of the Christian era. January 6, March 25, and December 25 were front-runners in the speculation; but May 20, April 19 or 20, November 17, and March 28 were all put forth and stoutly defended. About 245 A.D., Origen, one of the most prominent of all the early church fathers, argued against celebrating Jesus' birthday at all, sniffing "as if he were a king Pharaoh." December 25 was observed by pagan Romans as a feast day related to the sun; and pre-Christian era Britons observed December 25 as Mother's Night. Because of the winter solstice, falling on December 21 or 22, when the days begin to be longer with daily increase of light and decrease of darkness, and there was universal recognition of this major natural phenomenon, there came to be gradual acceptance of December 25 as an acceptable new feast day when the birth of Jesus could be appropriately celebrated. Roman Catholics set aside the four Sundays prior to December 25 as the "Advent season" ending with their midnight Eucharist, Christ's mass. Thus the term Christmas metamorphosed over nearly two thousand years to become what it is today.

The associations related to Christmas which I find most deeply embedded in my psyche are those formed when I was quite young: a well-formed but always smallish cedar tree cut from our own woods, a very few little packages (remember that this was in the heart of the Great Depression), fine, big fires in our living room fireplace, stockings stuffed with apples and oranges, nuts, and a few pieces of candy, and lots of wonderful food -- chicken and dressing, mashed potatoes and gravy, cranberry sauce, candied yams, hot biscuits, and homemade fruitcake. My best things, though, were the fireworks -- firecrackers, sparklers, and Roman candles.

Surely these are the kinds of things that Pope Gregory I must have had in mind with his reference to "outward pleasures." They certainly pleasured me.

And why not?

In his Christmas oratorio "For the Time Being," W. H. Auden has the Magi to say, "To learn to be human now is the reason we follow this star."

The magic of Christmas lets us affirm our humanity, the fruitcakes and firecrackers, the chicken and dressing, the mashed potatoes and hot biscuits, and all the other pleasures of hearth and home.

Oh, I suppose there will always be hair-shirted Puritans who want us to be miserable, to eat no fruit salad and to shoot off no firecrackers. These Grinches would, without a qualm, steal the fun and wonder of Christmas from little boys and girls, and from the rest of us as well. However, like Paul who knew not only how to be "abased" but also how to "abound," I am inclined at this Christmas season to the abounding option, learning better, like Auden's wise men, how "to be human now."

I invite you, then, to join me this Christmas to revel at the twinkling lights, to join in joyful singing of "Here Comes Santa Claus" and "Rudolph the Red-Nosed Reindeer," to read together again as my father used to read to me when I was a boy sitting in his lap, "Twas the night before Christmas . . . ," to indulge in a second helping of chicken and dressing, to throw another log on the fire, and to splurge by giving something extravagant to someone you really love. Salute the magic. Merry Christmas.

Now lest you slam judgment on me for being obscenely hedonistic, please stay tuned. .

Christmas is also miracle.

In Jesus Christ, God has become one of us. Identifying with us in the incarnation, the eternal Word of God has been made flesh, and the Reason of God has been thus expressed in a language that everybody can understand. As we are told in the beginning of the Gospel of John, God's light has shined in the darkness, enlightening everyone, and full of grace and truth so that in the miracle of Christmas we behold the glory of God Himself and are enabled to experience salvation, full and free which is God's gift to all who in repentance and faith come willingly to Him.

Christmas is the best time of the year.

Bask in its sunshine.

Warm by its fire.

Join in its Hallelujah Chorus.

Change

I HAVE A couple of friends who wake up every morning trying to think of things to change that day. No matter how well things have worked in the past, no matter how smoothly things are running now, and no matter how the status quo is humming along, their nostrils flare with the prospect of changing everything. Today if possible. If not today, then tomorrow for sure. Certainly no later than Friday of this week. Just run over anybody who gets in the way, or fire them, whichever comes first. But do get on with the change.

Me?

I just hate change.

One of the best things about God, it seems to me, is caught in a wonderful old hymn, "Abide with me," one stanza of which closes, "O Thou who changest not, Abide with me."

And one of the many good things about the Lord Jesus Christ is that he is "the same yesterday, and today, and forever" (Hebrews 13:8).

A little change is permissible, I suppose, if it comes slowly. For instance, the transition from one season of the year to the next is quite nice. The growth of a child from stage to stage and from year to year is about right. I also liked the really imperceptible growth of a great old spruce tree that grew by the side of our cabin in the mountains. This tree was at least 100 years old and 200 feet high when

I built the cabin by the river in 1958. Then the dreaded bud worms moved up the valley and killed that grand old tree. When we cut it down, I counted the tiny growth rings, one for each year of its life, on the stump and found that it had averaged growing less than an eighth of an inch in diameter for each of its 124 years of age. Watching it grow for the forty years I knew it was sort of like watching paint dry. Not all that dramatic. But quite satisfactory.

As I mentioned, I really do not like change, especially fast change or sudden change.

Whether we embrace change or resist it, however, change happens.

Adam is purported to have said to his wife as they left the Garden of Eden, "Well, Eve, we live in an age of transition."

In spite of my own aversion to change, I have hammered out a reasonably satisfactory way to deal with it.

When change comes, I try to fall back on Romans 8:28. All things are everlastingly working together for good to them that love the Lord and are called according to his purpose. At the time of unwelcome change, I have often felt in my bones that Brother Paul may have just blown it when he wrote that. But time and perspective have a way of validating it, time and time again.

Sometimes it is not possible to perceive any good in the change wrought by cruel fate. At such times, I have been known to fall back in mute despair in the realization that we live in a fallen world. Things simply do not always work out right. Troubles come as surely as the sparks fly upward. As a wise and wonderful grandmother I know said recently to a coddled grandchild who was whimpering because he had skinned his knee a little, "Get over it." There may be nothing else to do but to get over it.

Not many things in life are more solidly satisfying than

old shoes. Old hats pleasure me. Old and threadbare clothes move me to sighs of contented satisfaction. No less an eminence than Thomas Carlyle has observed that you should never trust the heart of a man for whom old clothes are not venerable. Old clothes, old hats, and old shoes, however, do wear out. I mean plumb out. Like my good neighbor's dearly loved old dog with massive arthritis and metasticized cancer so that she simply could not get on her feet anymore and was mercifully put to sleep by a sympathetic veterinarian, old clothes, too, pass their point of no return. Change is required. The new things are not really as satisfactory as the old. Given time, however, they too can become venerable.

Change can be the occasion for gratitude. Old age inevitably brings the loss of loved ones and old friends as it has been doing with unwelcome frequency to me in recent years. I have therefore often been moved to express deep gratitude to God for the many good times and the innumerable blessings extended to me by those who cared for me. As my vision dims, I am all the more grateful to God for all the beauty I have been privileged to see in days gone by. As hearing loss creeps up on me with little cat feet, I am moved to thanksgiving to God for marvelous whispers heard in the past, and for fine music's nuanced intricacies which I cannot now catch. As worldwide travel and glorious adventures are now not welcome or even tolerated, I am now doubly appreciative to the Giver of all good and perfect gifts for those incredibly good times in the past when I have been there and done that.

Change is a reminder that though the mills of God grind slowly, they grind exceedingly small. God's people, his kind of folks, may be perfectly confident in the knowledge that all creation, though now groaning and in travail, is tending toward a fruition, a fulfillment, a consummation that is far better than anything we now know or think.

Furthermore, and to dredge up a modicum of honest candidness in what has been something of a diatribe against change, I vigorously affirm change as being sometimes greatly needed. I think of human slavery, the systemic abuse of women, child labor, political corruption, economic oppression of the poor, rape of the environment, genocide, religious persecution, the trashing of the public schools, rampant gambling, the coddling of alcohol and tobacco profiteers, and family disintegration. Indeed, I have spent the last fifty years of my life focused on this motto, "Helping changed people to change the world." That engraved motto rests prominently on my desk today.

Yes, I do hate change.

Except when it is the most important thing on earth to do.

Fishing

UNLIKE THE AVID fisherman who was dressing to go to church on Sunday morning and while absent-mindedly tightening his necktie with the necessary tugs suddenly fancied that he had a fine fish on his hook and jerked so hard that he choked himself to death, I myself have never been caught up in fishing.

Nevertheless, fishing pleasures me.

While I can take it or leave it, I'd really rather take it.

For instance, just this morning, quite early, I had an inordinately pleasant dream that I had gone fishing. The lake was calm. A light wind from the south was at my back as I ambled around a little bay looking for a likely place to try my luck. The early morning sun was at my back and a few fleecy clouds floated desultorily overhead. A particularly attractive patch of water caught my fancy and I put down my beat-up old tackle box with a fine feeling that this might very well be their address. A medium-sized lure was chosen and snapped into place. My first cast was a little short; and the second was pulled off unsatisfactorily to the left. The third try was on target, at least close enough for government work. The lure had sunk well out of sight when something hit it like a ton of bricks, in the most gloriously thrilling experience a fisherman can be convulsed with. I set the hook and, nostrils flared, started reeling in my unknown quarry. The lake bank at that point was not satisfactory for landing a fish so I sidled my way to the right about 30 or 40 feet while slowly taking up as much slack as I dared without breaking the line or losing the fish. When it had tired a little, I backed up until I caught a glimpse of the beauty and was able then to drag him up on the grass. Boy and man—I've fished a long time, but never have I seen such a member of the finny tribe as this. It was nearly two feet long, full bodied, astoundingly active, and beautiful to behold. Its coloring was yellowish brown with a white underside, mottled like a tabby cat, and a snow-white tail section. It was like no other fish I have ever seen. I will never know its true pedigree, however, for at that moment I woke up, much too exhilarated to go back to sleep. The dream was wonderfully vivid, in gorgeous technicolor, and its images are indelibly fixed in my mind.

In my day I've caught my share of catfish and perch (not to mention crawfish, heavy-bodied and deep-voiced bull frogs, and an occasional cottonmouth moccasin gigged at night with a steel gig and a good flashlight) from the tank below our barn at my boyhood home. With catalpa worms for bait, I've hauled many a channel catfish into a boat over East Texas lakes. Trolling about 30 feet deep in Coal Lake not far from Mt. McKinley in Alaska, where fish and wildlife authorities assured us there were no fish whatsoever, I've caught marvelous salmon-fleshed rainbow trout, one whopper 22 1/2 inches long!

But the mountain streams and small lakes of the Sangre de Cristo Range in northern New Mexico have brought me more sheer delight than all my other fishing experiences put together. There have been rainbow trout, fat native brook trout, native cutthroat trout, an occasional German Brown trout, and now and then a rare Rio Grande trout, gloriously and uniquely red-bellied and splendidly delicious when fried to perfection. The rushing mountain streams are best for me; but at 9,000 to 10,000 feet altitude, there are so many trees and bushes at the edge of the water and over the water that fly fishing can be done only with great difficulty. Salmon eggs and worms are better for me; and the streams provide a good trout hole about every 30 yards or so. High mountain lakes provide a diversion and offer the added incentive of breathtakingly beautiful mountain scenery that is second to none in all the world. And the fish hooked there are almost invariably jumpers, adding immeasurably to the sport.

Of course, there is a bit of a downside to fishing. Under certain circumstances including appropriate climatic conditions, a fish out of the water will stink. Also when you are unhooking them they can fin you without a qualm leaving a painful infection that can persist for days. Then I am loath to recall how many hooks I have lodged in my poor clothes, not to mention my poor body—fingers, hands, legs, and once a hapless ear. Hanging your hook in a tree limb over the water can be an exasperating experience, especially when you have just missed a big one after a vigorous strike. Preparing the gear is nearly always aggravating, particularly when you know you left it in tip-top shape and a raucous young grandson has come along and trashed it to the max. Furthermore, the flesh of a fish may well be the most expensive meat you can ever expect to eat.

Still . . . still, a body keeps going fishing.

Especially when under some weight like Peter who, after the Lord's crucifixion, simply allowed to his fellow disciples, "I'm going fishing" (John 21:3). Or like one of the greatest Christian statesmen of the last century, Dr. J.M. Dawson, who was told by his medical doctor, "You can maintain your present schedule and die within a couple of years or you can take off one day a week and go fishing and expect to live another 20 years." Dr. Dawson took the good doctor's good advice and lived well into his nineties, having fished up to the very end.

Please excuse me now.

I simply have to go.

Fishing.

Turtles Do

A CERTAIN REPTILIAN somnolence engulfs me, body and soul, in the warm sunshine of a mid-winter afternoon. My study is on the west side of our house; and a wall of glass, twelve feet by eight feet, provides the greatest possible exposure to the output of the sun, the smallish nuclear furnace which sustains all the life there is on this third rock out from the fire. Delicious. Simply delicious.

Turtles, which crave this very same warmth, will crowd themselves onto a floating log and there, side by side, soak up this wonderful sunshine. They are responding to the same prurient yearning for warmth and light that compels me to keep returning to this marvelous place in my study. For all the tea in China, however, I wouldn't tump myself off into the cold water like the turtles do when startled. I just want to be left alone on my special log, soaking up the sunshine.

Are we kin to turtles? Why are our nervous systems extraordinarily similar to those of frogs? Why do placental creatures like female humans have 28-day cycles of ovulation, corresponding precisely to the waxing and waning of the moon, the moon with its magic light, the moon with its magic spells, the moon with its magic tides? Why must a human being stay very, very close to the norm of 98.6 degrees Fahrenheit in body temperature in order to stay alive? Why must we humans adhere very closely to our natural circadian rhythms of 24 hours, the time it takes our globe to rotate, or be seriously maladjusted and ultimately unable to function? Why have the human genome projects determined that human beings and chimpanzees have some 98 percent of the very same DNA? Why, indeed? Hm-m-m-m-m-m.

In recent times considerable amounts of energy, time, and money have been expended in pressing for what is generally called Creationism on the one hand or what is generally called Darwinian evolution on the other hand. Creationism has many faces and a wide variety of followers but may be generally understood to mean a world-view based on a literal interpretation of the method thought to have been used by God to create the world and all that is in it, the universe and all that is in it. Creationists and Intelligent Design adherents distinguish themselves from atheistic rationalists who pooh-pooh the notion of "intelligent design" and are adamant in refusing to allow God a place in their scheme of things. They want natural selection without God to be the explanation of creation and are just as rigid and pridefully arrogant in pressing for their "without God" beliefs as Creationists and Intelligent Design people can be in pressing for their "with God" doctrines.

Well, I just don't think I have a dog in this fight. I think I choose not to get caught up in this either-or debate where each side despises the other, denigrates the other, castigates the other, and treats the other with vitriolic contempt if not genuine hatred.

Come, let us reason together.

If God chose to use the slow method of evolution for the creating of the world and the universe, I cannot understand why it should confound the Creationists or the Intelligent Design people. Is God's arm shortened so that He can not reach across eons of time and infinite space? Is His work schedule limited so that He is required to behave Himself according to our puny definitions and formulations and charts and diagrams and calendars? Are we to think that He must have acted in creation so as to protect the empires or enterprises or theses of either naturalistic rationalists or rationalistic supernaturalists whose special turfs both seem quite prepared to fight and die for?

I think not.

Must God Almighty's "day" mentioned in Genesis be defined by our dime store watches?

Give me a break.

If God chose to use natural selection as one of His tools in His work of creation, what atheist can prove scientifically that He did not do so? Who knows what the finger of God stirring around in the primordial ooze could have started?

It is a faith-based conviction for me that in the beginning God created the heavens and the earth; and I don't care a fig if He used natural selection across eons of time to do it. It is an anti-faith-based conviction for the no-God naturalist that God did not do it. I like my faith better than his anti-faith. He likes his anti-faith better than my faith. I like my acceptance of Genesis 1:1, "In the beginning God..." better than his plaintive "In the beginning..."

Why fuss about it? We are disagreed. It is neither productive nor profitable for us to keep beating this horse.

When God said, "Let there be light," it is unlikely that He said it in English with an East Texas accent as I would. Most scientific theorists now seem to be inclined to think that time and space and the universe and all that is in it started with a "Big Bang" some 13.5 to 15 billion years ago. Exactly *how* God did this, I have to tell you I just do not know; and exactly *how* He struck the match that kindled the fire in the sun and started the light to burning, I do not know. But I am remembering the wise words of my old theology professor, Dr. W.T. Conner, "It's better not to know so much than to know so much that isn't so."

If I see "intelligent design" in the marvels of the human eye and accept the possibility that God used billions of years of natural selection to perfect this incredibly complex and altogether marvelous work, then who is the atheistic naturalist to put me down and gainsay what I see or who is the Creationist to put me down or gainsay my willing acceptance of the idea that God's method of creation could be the method of natural selection?

Many, many books have been written about all of this. Even more articles have flooded learned journals about it, especially in recent years. The Public Broadcasting System recently presented a seven-part series entitled "Evolution" with a final section on "What about God?" Furthermore, the *New York Review of Books* recently carried a long two-part essay, "Saving Us from Darwin," by Frederick Crews, a literary scholar from the University of California at Berkeley, in which he intemperately attacks Christians and Christianity while haughtily displaying an indefensible bias toward a Godless creation and a Godless world-view. *The Christian Century* responded by carrying a substantive article by Boston College professor Stephen J. Pope on "Christ and Darwin" in which he countered much of the PBS material and refuted the Crews essay's "emotionally driven materialistic ideology to steamroll distinctions, to propound grossly inaccurate historical generalizations, to mistake nuance and subtlety for evasion and rationalization, to introduce ad hominem accusations in place of reasoned arguments, to equate Sunday School catechism with systematic theology, and to beguile people into thinking they face a forced choice between two simplistically formulated and mutually exclusive options—Christ or Darwin."

I think it would be better if the whole lot would bask in the winter sunshine "while it is day, ere the night cometh."

Turtles do.

Now, if I've disturbed you a little, I'm glad.

I'm too old to mess around with things that aren't controversial.

❧ Sounds of the Season ☙

THE SOUNDS OF Christmas started early this year.

Bent on evoking the warm fuzzies of the Christmas season, advertisers have sought to ensnare us with snatches of "White Christmas," "Rudolph," "Sleigh Bells," "Joy to the World," and "Silent Night" and then lead us, like lambs to the slaughter, to buy their pricey baubles. This clever ploy, however, has led me not to succumb to their blandishments but to conjure up a flood of happy recollections of the sounds of the season.

I have been remembering the crackling and gently hissing sounds of the burning Yule logs, the fine kitchen sounds of my Mother's busy activity in preparing the feasts of the holiday season, the lowing of the cattle coming in from the pasture for the night and the barn's welcome protection from the whistling "Blue Northers," the chunking sound of a wheelbarrow full of firewood being piled on the porch to keep the fire going through the long winter nights, the welcome noisiness of visiting kinfolks and exuberant children and good neighbors dropping by to share a mess of fresh pork ribs or a jar of homemade preserves or just to sit a spell and rock and visit, and, of course, the old Christmas songs sung together in church, the same year after year in a truly authentic liturgy. Memories of these sounds of the season are special. Very special.

Move with me now to a more generic consideration of sounds.

I was actually launched into this line of thought by one of nature's most wonderful symphonies.

A big V-shaped flock of Canadian geese had just flown over our house, honking with such unfettered abandon as to wake the dead. Why such noisy chattering I do not know. I wish I did. Nature does not customarily waste such a precious commodity as the breath of life, so there was to be a reason for this glorious conversation of these marvelous birds. Maybe it is just because they are gregarious and crave conversation. Flying at speeds of up to sixty miles per hour at altitudes of up to three thousand feet, these great snow white geese can travel several hundred miles a day, honking all the way. Their migration over the house where I now live, has reminded me of a hundred such soundings, by night and by day, remembered from my childhood where we lived directly under a major flyway of migratory fowl. What a splendid déja vu. Lovely, indeed.

A grocery store serendipity a few days ago turned my motor over in a most delightful way. A one-year old seductress absolutely captivated me with her remarkably humanoid verbalizations. The encounter was on this wise. Her mother had stopped the big grocery cart in which this happy little person was ensconced. She had rather short reddish hair and unbelievably bright blue eyes. Her mother was occupied with putting away her credit cards and rumbling around in her purse for her keys. I stooped down to look directly into this little girl's eyes and then spoke sincerely and pleasantly to her. She smiled broadly baring two glistening front teeth extremely well lubricated with her very own saliva and broke into an astounding utterance of pre-speech, one of the most amazing phenomena of human development. Speech as such had not yet come to this little person, but it was obviously not far away. Hers was a first draft of words just about to form and erupt. After this pleasant outburst succeeded almost immediately by yet another ecstatic communication with a passing grandfatherly type of old man, she clammed up and again smiled sweetly as her mother wheeled her away to their car. She is gone but the melody of her speech lingers on, a lovely sound if ever I heard one.

One of the most memorable sounds of my entire lifetime came to me not long ago in the high mountains of the Sangre de Christo Range in northern New Mexico. Our Number One daughter had insisted on taking me as her guest for a jeep-enabled jouncing high country safari. In due time we drove quietly up on a great herd of cow elks, grazing with their nursing young calves close beside them, an elk nursery we later came to understand. When the herd, at least a hundred of them we reckoned, became suspicious of us, they started moving away, quite slowly at first; but then they broke into a trot and then into a dead run. Coming to a formidable barbed wire fence, the cows jumped it with unseemly grace, hardly slowing down.

The calves, however, had to stop and crawl under the fence or between the wires, in the process becoming separated from their mothers. The cows, gregarious by nature, reconnoitered behind the first nearby knoll which was covered by a dense growth of fir and young blue spruce trees, well hidden from us. As we waited to watch the last few straggling calves negotiate their passage through the fence, we began to hear the cows calling.

Now a bull elk bugles or trumpets with a decidedly masculine tone; but elk cows have a much more lady-like voice, not unlike the guttural whimper of a hungry puppy. Imagine a hundred elk cows gently calling, each with her own distinctive small female bugle voice which her own calf could recognize. We listened in profound wonder. It was a symphony of such wild and natural beauty as human ears could ever hope to hear. Finally the last stray calf was united with its mother and the symphony ended. It was a once-in-a-lifetime audience that can only be remembered as truly blessed.

Then there are the recollected sounds of huge bullfrogs croaking their wonderful love songs and perhaps declaring their territoriality from the banks of the nearby tank when I was growing up; the whippoorwill's beautifully unique "chip-flew-out-of-the-white-oak" call on an early summer evening as the night was settling in; the hoot owl's gentle invitation to camaraderie extended to one of his own kind from the upper limbs of a great old post oak near my upstairs bedroom windows in the still of the night; and the Bob White's crisp, bold call to another of his species responding from some unseen fence post some distance away.

Join me, then, in celebrating sounds in general and the blessed sounds of the Christmas season in particular. Sound is the gift of God; and hearing has to be one of God's most marvelous contributions to our human happiness and well being. Among all our Christmas gifts this season, I hope we can join in breathing a prayer of thanksgiving for all the sounds that signal God's great grace.

Merry Christmas.

❡ Stoking and Poking ❡

WINTER'S GRIP HAS been firm again this year. It usually is. I deal with it grudgingly and sometimes grouchily. One of my best but not very clever or innovative ways of dealing with it is by building a good fire in my big wood-burning fireplace in my blessed study.

Just today I have been contemplating my blessings while sitting in front of this fire which I have kept stoked and poked since very early morning. Some of these blessings have not exactly overwhelmed me but have instead slipped up on me, sidling in, dropping down, and even creeping up from behind. Some may be worth sharing.

The Fire Itself. Since time immemorial fire has been one of our most treasured human possessions, one of life's most basic necessities, about as rudimentary as food, clothing, and shelter. Our ancestors, of course, did not invent fire. After lightning would strike a tall tree or after a volcano would erupt with a fearsome flow of red hot molten lava, I suppose our forebears readily enough found that they were significantly more comfortable with the fires that had been started than they were without them. Then I suppose they began to tend the fire, to nurture it, and to guard it. When the weather was cold neighbors would share a few live coals with which their friends could rekindle their own fires that had inadvertently been allowed to go out. Early on, ingenious persons around the world devised ways and means of starting fires, using sticks rubbed together, flint rocks, or twirled points in a bed of dry moss. Matches were not invented until very recent times. The Encyclopedia Britannica says that the first practicable friction match was marketed in 1827. That is when my great grandfathers and grandmothers were already grown young men and women. My particular fire before which I am now sitting was started with an ingenious little propane torch costing about $3 which, when triggered, lights a natural gas starter which in turn quickly catches my wood on fire. Presto. I have fire in my fireplace.

Hearth and home have long gone together. In the old days home without a hearth would hardly have been imaginable. When I was growing up 75 years ago, my mother, on a bitterly cold winter day when it was simply too cold to fire up the kitchen stove on the north side of our drafty two storied house, would prepare a big black iron pot of hominy which she would cook for a very long time over a big bed of hot coals raked out from the fireplace in our living room to the edge of the hearth. Then at suppertime when the hominy was deliciously tender she would rake out more live coals onto the hearth and on these would cook a hoecake, biscuit dough formed into one big, flat portion. When fully cooked and beautifully browned, broken into pieces and generously buttered, it became with hot hominy, a meal fit for the gods. Ah, hearth and home, indeed.

Thank God for the fire itself.

Warm Feet. Once the fire is going, there is nothing so delicious on a really cold winter day when there is a heavy cloud cover hanging low overhead, than to prop your feet on the raised hearth, happily built of rough sandstone to about fifteen inches in height, and there leave them until they are toasty warm. Even when I was a boy, I remember how much I liked putting my feet, as often as not wet and cold, in front of the fire and leaving them there until the numbness of the cold was all gone and the warmth of my newly blessed feet had osmosed to the rest of my happily thawing self. Now that I am old, the former pleasure of really warm feet seems to have been multiplied exponentially. So, thank the Lord for warm feet; and may your own feet be warmed by whatever fire you can relate to when winter's fierce blasts come your way.

A Warm Back Side. Nothing, absolutely nothing, is more profoundly satisfying than backing up to a good, warm fire on a really cold winter day. City slickers who grew up with space heaters, floor furnaces, or central heat can always be identified by their unseemly awkwardness in front of a winter fire. They seem incapable of grasping the elemental importance of *backing up* to the fire instead fronting up to it. (There is a downside to this stance, however. If a body has a big, older brother, he can come up and catch the front part of your britches and pull them smartly so that the inordinately hot pants legs next to the fire are brought into painful contact with the tender calves of both legs. This unholy maneuver requires a little time and a good deal of grace before fraternal relations can be smoothed out and the fire can once again be backed up to.) It is my belief, based on long observation, that real men and women will always spend about as much time backed up to a fire as they do facing it. I just think you can trust the heart of a man who backs up to a fire.

Flickering Firelight. The dancing flames of a fine wood

fire are authentically lovely, nothing short of truly beautiful. The aesthetic value of the fire is one of its primary benefits. A fire is admirable in its early stages when the flames are just beginning to lick the logs and get hold of the wood which they mean soon to devour. A fire is more wonderful still when it moves toward its maximum blazing and is coming to the zenith of its marvelous powers. Then when it has passed the height of its blazing, the fire comes to what is to me its most exquisite stage with a full complement of glowing coals, red hot, some almost white hot, with just a little white and gray ash beginning to form as the embers prepare to fade away and finally die. The whole life cycle of a fire is a thing of beauty and a joy forever, a phenomenon to wax lyrical about.

Aroma Therapy. On two occasions lately, I have been in shopping malls where I have walked up on aroma therapy salons. I gather that these enterprises are trying to make money by hawking scents, perfumes, sprays, smells, odors, and sundry aromatic offerings. Good idea, I suppose. Actually, however, I can think of few things that could be more pleasing to the olfactory nerves than the subtle odors of burning wood. One of the main reasons for having a wood fire is to enjoy the delicate cachets of different kinds of wood as they burn, pinyon being a prime example. A smoking fireplace is, of course, an abomination. When a poorly built chimney does not draw properly, smoke pours out into the room, burns the eyes, offends the nose, and antagonizes the whole household. I am thankful that the builder of our house used an experienced and knowledgeable subcontractor to build our two wood burning fireplaces for they are constructed in such a way that neither of them has smoked a single time in the sixteen years that we have lived here. When a wood fire is burning, however, a delicate, unobtrusive, but splendidly pleasing aroma can be detected. It is therapy.

Little Sounds. Separation from God is sometimes spoken of in the Bible as being cast into outer darkness and Jude calls the ungodly "wandering stars, to whom is reserved the blackness of darkness forever." One thinks of silence. Blaise Pascal, the French philosopher, theologian, and mathematician, has spoken of the eternal silences of the infinite spaces. There is a certain profundity about silence. Sound, however, is profounder still. God Himself is Word according to John 1:1, reason expressed in a language that humans can understand. God communicates with us through spoken words, through sung words, and through written words in his special Book. Do not judge me to be out of touch with reality now if I put forward an opinion that the little sounds made by a good fire may be heard by those with ears to hear as one of the languages of heaven. When there is green wood burning, a very special spewing, blowing, or even whistling can be easily heard. A piece of green hickory wood which has been coaxed to vigorous burning by several pieces of dry oak and a couple of small pieces of dry ash is capable of producing marvelous little musical notes which are beautiful and gloriously unique. A certain amount of dignified small popping is quite welcome, also. I especially enjoy the phenomenon called "popping snow" which can occasionally be heard. The churlish, raucous popping of fir, green or dry, however, is to be avoided if at all possible because it will both scare the living daylights out of you and wake up your wife in the nearby bedroom where she is trying to catch another little nap in the early morning when you have braved the elements by dawn's early light in order to get the fire going and drive the chill away before breakfast.

Mostly though the little sounds speak comfort, peace, happiness, and warmth, at least to me.

Reverie. A comfortable chair in front of a nice fire blazing away in a good fireplace is the quintessential matrix for reverie, which I understand to be the art of being lost in thought. It is near to being a lost art, of course; but I reckon that reverie is one of the fundamental building blocks of a healthy psyche. In these times we are so hurried by agendas that are too full, so harried by assignments, obligations, tuggings, and deadlines that we are hard pressed even to pause long enough to draw a deep breath. Sabbaths are not kept. Sleep is slighted. Rest is denied. Reverie is hardly in our vocabularies.

To sit alone in front of a good fire is to encourage contemplation. To stare at the coals as the fire burns down is to inject into the day's experience a solid quietness. To grow warm by the fire is to aid and abet the inclination to be still and know "that God is, and that he is a rewarder of them that diligently seek him" (Hebrews 11:6). To doze a little in the company of a warm fire is to relax in the deep knowledge that things are working together for good for those who love God and are called according to his purpose (Romans 8:28).

The ancient Greeks thought that fire was a very special possession of the gods and that it could be shared only grudgingly with mortals. With a different take on it, however, I understand fire to be one of God's good gifts, a not inconsequential component of his gracious provision for the abundant life.

And if all this doesn't light your fire, maybe *your* wood is wet.

Trivial Pursuits

FOR MOST OF my life, I have worked too hard, too long, and too much. I never got much into games. The more the pity. Since retirement, however, I have made it my business to set aside an hour or so after supper almost every single day to spend with Mary Louise, my wonderful wife of 56 years, for playing a rousing game of Scrabble. She enjoys it and so do I. It would be easy for me to feel guilty about this indulgence, to think that it is a foolishness that ought not to be embraced seeing that there is so much stuff that ought to be read, so much stuff that ought to be studied, so much stuff that ought to be cleared off my desk, and so much stuff that ought to be done in the house, around the house, in the garage, and to the yard. I keep playing Scrabble with Mary Louise, though, for I did not give her anywhere near as much time as I ought to have done for the first 40 or 50 years of our married life, and because I have finally found out that too much work and not enough play, as the old saying might be revised to go, "makes Jack a dull old dodder."

At the risk of offering irrefutable proof that I need to be put away in some institutional environment where I will do no harm to others or to myself, let me share with you some of the trivial pursuits that are now pleasuring me and may possibly be enriching my life. I can now take a little satisfaction in relishing things heretofore denied, put off, glossed over, rushed through, or callously rejected.

(Apologies are no doubt in order to the inventors, manufacturers, and promoters of the neat game of Trivial Pursuit which our children used to play when they were much younger and still at home.)

Some of my more trivial pursuits come to mind.

Staring at the fire. It doesn't even have to be very cold to relish this trivial pleasure. When you sit up close in front of the fireplace and look at the fire, glassy-eyed and with your mind in neutral, you are vaguely aware that the fire is always changing, unfailingly beautiful, and somehow deeply satisfying. Moreover, it is dependably and happily finite for a wood fire is soon spent. And in retirement and old age, *soon* comes quickly.

Dozing in front of the television. This is light years ahead of watching it.

Dawdling over a freezer of fresh homemade peach ice cream. Scientific thoroughness must be assigned to the task of cleaning the dasher to make sure that no melting glob of the precious substance is allowed to be wasted. Then when your bowl is filled and then refilled, the corpus of this glorious concoction is to be mincingly and meticulously savored in the realization that probably no king of England ever could even have aspired to anything quite as exquisite. Trivial? Maybe. But still deserving of a ten-gun salute.

Listening to a roomful of uninhibited grandchildren. By my best estimate, I can hear only about one tenth of what they are saying, although heaven knows that it is not a problem caused by inadequate volume on their part. I am content to catch no more than a tithe of what is being said for I reckon that I have already heard most of what they are chattering about. And to tell the truth, I don't really give a fig about all the trivia. It is the overall experience that I like. Rattle on.

Watching nighthawks feeding on a summer evening. They are catching mosquitoes and high-flying insects over the brightly-lighted ballpark behind our house. The nighthawk is a marvelous creature. Some Europeans call these birds goat-suckers. (I'll tell you why some day when you have a little time.) My Daddy called them bullbats. They are astonishingly ugly, incredibly agile, and notoriously secretive. But in the summer night sky brilliantly lighted for the night ball games, scores of them present a fascinating spectacle with their soaring, turning, diving, and circling. Akin to the equally elusive whippoorwill (officially "nocturnal nightjars") these critters may be trivial, but I find them terrific.

Watching the lightning play at night in a distant thunderstorm. This common occurrence has been impressively presented by Mother Nature since time immemorial. I like the infinitely variable lightning streaks but my favorite part of the show is the sheet lightning that momentarily makes a brilliant spectacle of a towering thunderhead. This sight may be commonplace, even trivial, but I allow that it offers more variety and originality than television sitcoms.

Looking at the river. In more than 50 years of watching the little mountain stream on the banks of which I built a cabin in 1958, I have never seen the Red River flag or fade. It is always changing but always the same, always in a hurry yet always running at the same speed in obedience to the call of gravity that draws it down the mountain to the same old sea. Trivial but always fascinating.

Doing things with numbers. I have no idea why numbers are endlessly appealing to some of us; but certain people seem to get absolutely ecstatic when they see an automobile odometer present such a wonderful sight as 77,777.7 or 99,999.9 or 123, 456.7. In my case it calls for stopping the car and relishing the magic of the moment. I remember reading an article more than ten years ago in *The New Yorker* called "The Mountains of Pi" which told about two brothers named Chudnovsky who came to America from Kiev in Russia. These brilliant Russian Jews, Ph.D.s in mathematics, devoted their lives to what most people would consider the trivial pursuit of trying to fathom the apparently fathomless dimensions of Pi. As we may remember, Pi denotes the ratio of the circumference of a circle to its diameter. The ratio itself has a numerical value of 3.14. Those who are not mathematicians can be quite satisfied, thank you, with that number; but number theorists like the Chudnovskys happily spend their lives in pushing out the numbers not just past 3.14 to 3.14159265 but then on to the hundreds, then thousands, then millions, and then billions as they look for some pattern in this transcendental number which cannot be expressed by either arithmetic or algebra. Numbers addicts around the world, however, seem never to tire of searching with the most powerful computers on earth for the exact answer to what still seems, after thousands of years, to be an insoluble puzzle. Though I am an absolute novice in this field, I am myself intrigued by this search for exactitude, no matter how trivial the pursuit may seem to be.

These are all little things, trivial things, to be sure. Yet,

WHATSOEVER THINGS ARE LOVELY   133

Little drops of water,
Little grains of sand
Make the mighty ocean
And the pleasant land.

When you put together such little experiences, such trivial pursuits, you get a collage of memories and tap into a vast treasure trove of some of the best things in life. So...

Long live trivial pursuits. In a way, to use Brother Paul's word to the Philippians, "lovely," and well worth thinking on.

Funny How Time Gets Away

SOMETIMES TIME DRAGS.

The teenager waiting for his driver's license perceives time as his mortal enemy. The excited young child finds Christmas so long in coming that even the sun must be standing still in the heavens. The still classroom-bound young adult ready to go out and conquer the world, full of vinegar and spizzarinktum (if you were from Van Zandt County in rural East Texas, you wouldn't have to wonder about the meaning of that impressive word), it seems that tomorrow will never come. Shakespeare got the point when he had the weary Macbeth say to Seyton, the officer attending him, "Tomorrow, and tomorrow, and tomorrow, creeps in this petty pace from day to day to the last syllable of recorded time."

Yes; sometimes time drags.

Then again time flies.

This is one of those times for me.

For the seventeenth time since moving into the house where I now live, I am observing from my study's west-facing picture window the apparent movement of the sun from its setting place about 40 degrees south of due west to the end of its seasonal journey about 40 degrees north of due west. The very middle of this six-months' journey is called, as we have been told, the vernal equinox. Easter has been rather arbitrarily set as the first Sunday after the first full moon following this vernal equinox. Our central

Christian holiday is thus seen to be determined by the tilting of the earth on its axis so that the setting sun seems to move south to north and then back north to south, south to north, north to south with the changing seasons. Whereas that movement used to seem to me to drag along in agonizingly slow motion, it is now in a runaway mode, zip, zip, running north like a scalded dog as the days get longer and then turning around to tear back south with the days getting shorter and shorter. As I say, zip, zip. Slam bam, thank you ma'am.

A thousand years ago Omar Khayyam wrote, "The Bird of Time has but a little way to flutter—and the Bird is on the Wing."

And Willie Nelson has plaintively sung, "Ain't it funny how time gets away."

Of course he doesn't mean funny "ha ha" or funny peculiar. He means funny sobering, funny inexplicable, funny profound.

My old-man thoughts, prodded to the surface by this azimuthal movement, or rather this *appearance* of the seasonal movement of the sun, now turn naturally to time itself. Relativists have proposed that time is merely a fourth dimension of space; but this gets a little heavy for me. My *Encyclopedia Britannica* allows "that time is fundamental and there is nothing similar or simpler to compare it with." Right on.

Philosophical ponderings about such things tend to lead me off into water that is too deep. There comes to mind the classic definition that such philosophizing is like a blind man in a dark room searching for a black cat that is not there. So, I am inclined to take time for granted, glancing desultorily at my watch now and then and then consulting the calendar from time to time only to forget forthwith both the time and the date so as to miss important obligations, appointments, and opportunities. Could it be sure proof that I have passed my allotted fourscore years?

As only the fool says in his heart that there is no God (Psalm 14:1), so I feel that we need not foolishly posit the opinion that there is no such thing as time. Yet, who of us has not sung these mysterious words in *When the Roll Is Called Up Yonder*: "When the trumpet of the Lord shall sound and time shall be no more"? The songwriter clearly knew Revelation 10:6 where the angel standing astraddle of the land and the sea raises his right hand and swears by God "that there should be time no longer." The phrase can be translated in different ways; but we can nevertheless be reminded that eternity is defined as infinite time, unmeasurable time, endless time.

In my lifetime thus far, if I have figured this out with reasonable accuracy, my heart has beat already about 2,943,360,000 times. (If you want to know, I arrived at this numerical oddity by multiplying my average heartbeat rate of about 70 per minute times the 60 minutes in an hour times the 24 hours in a day times the 365 days in a year times my 80 years which I have lived thus far. Presto. About three billion beats.) No machine ever conceived by human minds or built by human hands comes anywhere near the efficiency or the longevity of this fantastic little pump, the human heart, about the size of a smallish grapefruit. But with its beats we number our days.

When there are no more beats left, there are no more days.

Time's up.

I have been contemplating our creaturely existence "when time shall be no more."

This is a profundity with which nearly everybody seems

to have wrestled: Solomon, Socrates, Newton, Einstein, and Thomas Wolfe with his *Of Time and the River*—and more recently Hawking, Pogo, Charlie Brown, and uncounted farmers, shepherds, disconsolate teenagers, long-haul truck drivers, and anxious, sleep-deprived mothers and fathers around the world distraught about their children.

Swimming in such deep waters may have some aerobic benefit for many, but I am personally more inclined to *floating.*

My friend Kenneth Chafin, redeeming the time, caught this floating concept in a moving piece he called "A Rhythm for My Life." I think he may have had some premonition of his approaching promotion to a better world. At least he had a finely mature awareness of the fleeting nature of time and the transience of the things of this world when he prayed to God

> Help me to find a rhythm for my life
>   in keeping with my strength, my gifts,
>   my opportunities, my commitments,
>   and thy larger purpose.
> Let there be a celebration of life,
>   the building of relationships,
>   and the nurturing of others.
> Let there be unhurried strolls in the woods,
>   quiet mornings spent on the pond,
>   poking around country roads,
> Afternoon naps in the porch swing,
>   leisurely meals with friends,
>   chickadees fed and zinnias grown.
> Let there come to me a quietness of soul,
>   a relaxed body, an alert mind,
>   a gentle touch, an inner peace,
>   an integrity of being.

It's time to do it.

As Snuffy Smith was wont to say, "Time's a-wastin'."

Summertime

SUMMERTIME IS THE BEST season of the year.

At least that's my take on it.

I was born in July, you know. So when the sun is really bearing down, the weather by day and by night is hot as blazes, and even the trees seem ready to lie down and pant, then everything seems to me to be in place just as it ought to be and "God's in his heaven: All's right with the world," as Robert Browning had Pippa, the quintessential Pollyana, to say.

No other season has such a wonderfully high-class song written about it: "That Good Old Summertime."

No other season is associated so warmly (get it?) with such a kaleidoscope of pleasant memories, particularly from childhood.

And no other season can claim such a wide and varied and exciting menu of lovely things to do, lovely places to go, and lovely fresh things to eat.

Consider ten especially good things about the summertime.

School Is Out. Whee! This is great for kids. They have been cooped up for nine interminable months and deserve the break. Teachers deserve a breather, too. When one college professor was asked what he liked best about his profession, he answered, "Three things: June, July, and August." Boys can go barefooted. Girls can spread out their dolls and play to their hearts' content. I have known one youngster, who later became a top-flight electrical engineer, who, when school was out, regularly climbed up in his favorite tree and read book after book after book through the summer.

Vacations. In asking friends and family, grandchildren, and neighbors what they liked best about the summertime, I got more votes for vacations than anything else. People like trips. We crave the open road. We relish the prospect of change, of new scenes, of new restaurants, of new places to picnic, and of making new acquaintances who could become new friends. Farmers like to slow down and relax in the knowledge that the crops are laid by. Frenchmen rush headlong like migrating wildebeests to distant watering holes. Urbanites flee from their cities. Country people head for theme parks. Kids who can, go to camps. Church choirs do their annual junkets. Preachers warm over their old sermons for the congregations are mostly gone anyway and won't be back until after Labor Day.

Family Time. The other seasons of the year seem so everlastingly filled with things to do that family time easily gets left to the last and then left out. Summer permits better priorities. Families travel together, go to see kinfolks together, go fishing together, watch Fourth of July fireworks together, make ice cream together, do watermelon cuttings together, watch summer sunsets together, search the night skies for falling stars together, and enjoy family cookouts together. This family togetherness is for me one of the very best things about summertime.

Catching Up. During the other seasons of the year, things

get put off. Reasonably important things get postponed so that attention can be focused on the most pressing things. Stuff requiring research, or reflection, or long distance telephone calls, or personal conferences get put in fat folders and pushed to a far side of the desk. Regular maintenance of all the machinery gets neglected and the squeaky wheel gets the grease. But summertime allows us to catch up, tie up the loose ends, and work through those stacks and files, doing those things that have to be done and throwing away those things whose deadlines have already passed. When summer's longer days and less hectic schedules allow us to clean off our desks, tidy up our garages, make those long delayed visits, and do those necessary runs to the hardware stores, we are rewarded with a warm and fuzzy feeling of achievement and inner peace. Thank the Lord for summer's provision of the chance to catch up.

Summer Sounds. Katydids, bullfrogs, hoot owls, whippoorwills, mockingbirds, and quails with their audaciously bold and emphatically clear bobwhite calls are among the marvelous symphonists of summertime. The softer sounds of summer breezes and hummingbirds, and turtledoves with their gently plaintive cooing are also wonderfully memorable. (By the way, did you know that "turtle" is the very old Old English word for "dove" so that we have the King James Version of the Song of Solomon 2:12 rendered, "the voice of the turtle is heard in our land"?) My own boyhood days on the farm were close to many sounds that seem now to be especially identified with the summertime: roosters crowing, hens clucking, chicks cheeping, guineas potracking, horses whinnying, cows mooing, and pigs squealing to signal that they knew it was feeding time—grunting contentedly when stretched out in the sun to be benignly scratched in the side with a handy corn cob in the hand of a kindly human.

Summer Flowers. Vivid colors, glorious blossoms, and exquisite aromas are all part of the show. There are a couple of marvelously fragrant roses in my own small rose garden now whose heady perfumes are enough to make a body walk sideways. The big magnolia tree's abundance of fantastic blooms that permeated the area around my upstairs bedroom where I slept until I went away to college is still vividly clear in my memory. Honeysuckles, of course, are commonplace but nonetheless appreciated. Trumpet vine blossoms, irises, zinnias, gardenias, lilacs, begonias, the clematis with its extravagant display of big and bold bright purple blossoms, mandevilla, impatiens, and crape myrtle all have unique niches to fill in a salute to summer flowers. One of my all-time favorites is a glorious field of blue gentians growing wild in unfettered profusion in a great open meadow at 9,000 feet altitude in the Sangre de Christo Mountains near Red River, New Mexico. Exquisite.

Summer Games. Baseball, of course, takes the cake. But softball, basketball, volleyball, and now soccer all have their special devotees. Touch football also draws its partisans into happy competition when a few friends have congregated and are physically able to run for a pass and then race, lumber, or lope for the back fence. Hide-and-go-seek is universally embraced and is best done in the summertime at dusk when the daylight is still lingering and the shadows of approaching night offer splendid places to crouch and avoid detection. My beloved wife of 57 years and I are happily content after supper with a rousing game of

Scrabble as the summer sun sinks toward a glorious sunset before fading peacefully into night.

Summer Gardens. Fresh vegetables and fresh fruits are in. They deserve a rousing cheer. Oh, I know about modern air-conditioned grocery stores with their produce flown in by refrigerated cargo planes from Chile and Australia and New Zealand and Israel and Costa Rica; and I am not ungrateful for this semi-fresh fare. The truth is, however, that these offerings cannot hold a candle to honestly vine ripened tomatoes, fresh corn pulled this morning, new potatoes, today's cutting of okra, sweet cantaloupes left on the vine until they are a solid sun-blessed yellow, and a ripe watermelon with a nice, green stem proving that this morning it happily nestled on the vine in its own watermelon patch. Furthermore, summer is, as far as I can determine, the God-ordained time to eat homemade fresh peach ice cream. Scraping the dasher is about as close as mortals are likely to get to the Elysian Fields of the Greek gods. Grilling out, moreover, is most happily done in the summertime. Whether the offering is chicken or hamburgers, steaks or wieners, ribs or shrimp, or marinated pork tenderloin. All offer special taste treats. My very best is pork chops slowly grilled to a golden brown with nothing added but a little salt and pepper and then tantalizingly enhanced with all beef wieners also slowly grilled until split open by the heat, right down the middle.

Summer Nights. A walk outside in the cool of the evening is an unforgettable experience on a summer night. The stars are twinkling, a blazing meteor can be an occasional serendipity, and a distant bank of thunder heads illuminated now and then by sheet lightening are all noteworthy. Summer fireflies work a magic of their own. Then it is nearly heavenly on a summer night to go to bed with the windows open so as to relish a pleasant south breeze coming through a nearby magnolia with its uniquely heady perfume embracing you as you drift off into lala land.

Summer Porching. (I am indebted to my friend Kyle Childress, pastor of the Austin Heights Baptist Church in Nacogdoches, Texas, for enabling me to name this delicious experience. He credits a friend from Louisville, Kentucky for giving him the name when he presented him with "a copy of a small coffee-table style book called *Porching: A Humorous Look at America's Favorite Pastime* by John H. Buchino, M.D., Professor of Pediatrics and Pathology at the University of Louisville School of Medicine.") To sit on the front porch and watch the world go by has to be one of summer's finest bequeathments to today's weary pilgrims. Especially after a hard morning's physical work and a hasty midday meal, a spell of porching can be just what the doctor ordered. A quick nap on a porch pallet can put icing on this cake. Another plus for porching is the rocking chair, for a little rocking can be our equivalent of what certain Hindu holy men do when they sit cross-legged on a tow sack and chant, "Om, Om, Om, Om" on and on. Although porching is something that has turned my motor over for as long as I can remember, now that I am in my really mature years, it has taken on a new aura of wondrous attraction. Please join me. I think it is not really necessary but you could ask your doctor if porching is right for you.

Why should these reflections about the good things of summertime have to end with ten? Just because God gave us ten digits on the ends of our arms, I suppose. Actually, there are many more reasons for saluting the summer season. I have written this less than scholarly treatise on the longest day of the year, however, and this is a reminder that all good things come to an end. Tomorrow the days will start getting shorter. Before we can catch our breaths, autumn will have come. Then the frosts will start. Then winter's icy grip will take hold. That will be the time to start looking toward spring. Then, presto, there will come once again "that good old summertime."

Imprecation for an Answering Machine

Breathes there a man
With soul so dead
Who never to himself
Hath said,

Curs't be that phone
On yonder end
Whose tape machine
My time doth spend.

With monotone
And silly choices,
"Press one; press two,"
The fool thing voices.

With patience gone
And anger hot
I wish this thing
Were not begot.

But since it's here
And I can't help it
Please bear with me
While I demean it.

"Press three; press four,"
It now is saying.

When it gets to seven,
I won't be staying.

Let those who will
Stay on the line
To hear them out
And stew and whine.

But as for me,
I've had enough.
They've missed my call
And that's just tough.

I'm hanging up
Though I'm loath to balk;
But I crave some human
With whom to talk.

When Ladies at the Lattice Lose Their Luster

OUR MORTAL LOT, according to the Psalmist (90:10), is to hope for a life span of some "three score years and ten." Then "by reason of strength" some may even attain "four score" years.

Strength or no strength, I attained that exalted status on July 3, 2003. It wasn't easy. It's still not.

You can tell you are 80:

When all your shoes are slow shoes;

When you've got more money than you have time;

When you never pass up an empty chair;

When everybody mumbles, mumbles, mumbles;

When you never remember a name but you always forget a face;

When you firmly agree with Thomas Carlyle's observation that you can never trust the heart of a man for whom old clothes are not venerable;

When you are nearly always ready to welcome "a little more sleep, a little more slumber, a little more folding of the hands to sleep" (See Proverbs 5:10 and 24:33). Ah. Yes. Tolstoy had it right to observe that a nap in the afternoon is silver, but that a nap in the morning is pure gold; and

When your daughter sends you a birthday card that says, "Dad, I hope you never lose your hair. It's such a nice one."

Solomon was an astoundingly insightful old man to write about the geriatric facts of life; and no one has rendered Ecclesiastes 12 as sensitively and as beautifully as James Moffatt:

> Remember your Creator in the flower of your age, ere evil days come on, and years approach when you shall say, "I have no joy in them;" ere the sun grows dark and the light goes from moon and stars, and the clouds gather after rain; when the guards tremble in the house of Life, when its upholders bow, when the maids that grind are few and fail, and ladies at the lattice lose their luster, when the doors of the street are shut, and the sound of the mill runs low, when the twitter of birds is faint, and dull the daughters of song, when old age fears a height and even a walk has its terrors, when his hair is almost white, and he drags his limbs along, as the spirit flags and fades.

Brother Solomon was singing my song.

Eighty is a sobering milestone. In addition to the grace of God, I have my rather long-lived forebears to thank for this modest achievement. I take precious little credit. A few things come to mind, however, as being possible contributors to the attainment of this mark. Please consider a few of them.

The hand of God. Deliverance from a lifetime of close calls which unbelievers might callously attribute to blind chance, or dumb luck, or immutable fate, I firmly believe to have been at the hand of the Lord. Near drownings, a copperhead snake-bite, sundry airplane crises such as engine failures over the open ocean and once over the vast expanse of the Amazon jungle, teenage idiocies, fearful food poisonings in primitive third-world preaching places, and two absolutely terrifying 2 a.m. batterings on my isolated, working-class hotel door when I was in St. Petersburg in the USSR teaching Christian social ethics to about forty of the finest and most earnest Christians I have ever encountered. My host, the seminary president, assumed it was KGB terrorists or hostile Russian Orthodox Church hit men or both. As we often sing, "Through many dangers, toils, and snares I have already come; 'Tis grace that brought me safe thus far, and grace shall lead me home."

Family. Fine parents and a good and faithful big brother, a wonderful wife for 56 years, three splendid daughters, and a gaggle of well-above-average grandchildren all have contributed significantly to my long life.

Friends. Not only would my life have been infinitely poorer without an extraordinarily wide circle of really good friends, but I am reasonably sure it would have been shorter. I know it would have been of a much poorer quality.

God's calling. An unwavering, unambiguous, unshakeable sense of God's special calling has kept my frail raft afloat. My feet have been often, if not nearly always, wet; but the raft has not yet sunk.

Sleep. Sleep has always come easily to me. Indeed, I have a perverse inability to stay awake when I am tired and stretched out. When normal people are tossing and turning, wide-eyed, stressed out, and weighed down with the cares of this world, I am zonked out in the mindless bliss of deep sleep. I hardly ever require more than about three minutes to drift off into deep sleep.

A cabin in the mountains. When I was about thirty years old, I found a piece of land at Red River, New Mexico, at 9500 feet altitude, some twenty feet from a trout stream, in a beautiful valley of blue spruce and quaking aspen. I borrowed every dollar of the money to buy it and then built a little cabin on it in 1958. For 45 years now this marvelous mountain retreat has been a life-renewing, battery-charging, soul-rejuvenating blessing.

Hard work. My hard work routine is a life pattern that I learned from my parents. One of my father's often-repeated admonitions was, "Hard work never killed anybody." While I had many occasions to think him mistaken about that hard saying, I am now confident that the strong medicine of hard work has significantly contributed to the quality as well as to the length of my life.

Leanness. For their good, God "sent leanness" to his sometimes rebellious, complaining, idolatrous people (Psalms 106:15). For most, affluence is a heavy burden which tends to bring stresses, anxieties, and unnumbered worries. The Great Depression with its terrible "Leanness" was probably the most defining experience of my life, not just affecting but actually shaping the first two or three decades of my life. Then when I finished my formal education at age 25, not much changed. Leanness kept hounding my hapless heels. After 7 years as the Director of the Texas Baptist Christian Life Commission (I was making $10,700 annually), when the Southern Baptist Christian Life Commission called me, the trustees strained mightily and matched that salary with not one penny of increase. Not to worry. The "leanness" has kept falling out for my good. I am compelled to salute it.

Banana pudding. There must be powerful karma in really good banana pudding. In my unscientific opinion, there are life-buoying elements literally teeming in a large bowl of hot banana pudding liberally sprinkled with nutmeg. A couple of scoops of Blue Bell Homemade Vanilla ice cream may be happily permitted but are not required. After all, it is hard to gild the lily.

Laughter. God gave me an abnormally exuberant and ready sense of humor. Things often strike me as funny. I guess I laugh more than most folks. A new joke mandates a long distance call to my brother and to selected friends. Repartee comes readily, and sometimes detrimentally, to my mind. Through all these years this good medicine has lifted my spirits, cleared my head, regulated my heartbeat, and eased my pains. I think it has prolonged my life.

Well, there you are.

Eighty. I did it. And I'm glad. A little surprised. But glad. Even though along the way, as Moffatt's translation puts it, the ladies at the lattice lost their luster. Or at least a right smart of it!

The Shade
at the End of the Row

THIS IS A CHEERFUL word about cemeteries.

Actually it is mostly about a special cemetery.

I've been there a hundred times.

Just visiting of course.

I speak of the graveyard by the meeting house of my home church, the Pleasant Union Baptist Church in East Texas about five miles north of Edgewood and a mile or so this side of the Sabine River.

The great old post oaks around the back of the meetinghouse, extending out over the cemetery, are probably well over two hundred years old. They are the very ones my deacon Daddy used to tie our team to when we pulled up our wagon and got out to go to the church services where my Mother taught Sunday School and he led the singing. (You might very well have found yourself in a fistfight if you had called him a Minister of Music or, heaven forbid, a Worship Leader. For crying out loud!) After our car was sold and our family settled into the grinding poverty of the Great Depression, that narrow-tired wagon and those two mules, Red and Steve, were our only means of getting around. Otherwise we walked. Like everybody else.

But I digress.

The cemetery never was a depressing place to me. It's still not. It was part of life. A part of church. A part of community. A part of family. Buried there are grandparents, aunts and uncles, cousins, early settlers, scalawags, bootleggers, heroes and heroines, godly old men and saintly old women, folks who would certainly have been candidates for beatification if dyed-in-the-wool Baptists and Methodists had dabbled in such a popish practice. And buried there are my parents and, next to them our blue-eyed and blond five-year old daughter.

When I walk those grounds, as I often do, I do so in profound sobriety.

I nearly always stop in solemn retrospection by the grave of Clarence Spradlin. Clarence got religion in his mature years, and he used to come faithfully to the stated services held in the one-room frame church house not thirty yards from where he is now resting. He faithfully carried a big, black Bible. He always wore high-mileage blue overalls. He never wore shoes. Summer and winter he never wore shoes. He didn't have any shoes. Trapping for mink and lesser game through those rugged creek and river bottoms, his bare feet got so calloused that you could easily strike a match on the bottom of either bare heel. I've done it lots of times. No "reed shaken by the wind," never cumbered with "soft raiment," not even remotely near being "gorgeously attired" (Matthew 11:8; Luke 17:24-28), Clarence Spradlin was the nearest man to John the Baptist I have ever known. With his kind of nerve, style, and smarts, he might well, under more fortuitous circumstances, have been an Amos, a Governor, a Senator, a rocket scientist, or an astronaut. He died when he was not yet forty.

Then I seldom fail to stop a while at the grave of Kenneth Jackson, a grand and godly old deacon whose words of encouragement and blessing spoken to me privately and with palsied deliberation right after I, as a boy, had publicly professed my faith in Jesus Christ as my personal Lord and Savior, still lodge in my mind after nearly seventy years.

The grave of a neighbor and an old family friend, Charlie Waggoner, is made special by a loving tribute, likely posted there by a grateful and caring daughter. The message is carried in a neat little sign by a blue plastic telephone, "Jesus Called Daddy Home." No, it is hardly on the same website as Shakespeare's Sonnets. But it is light years ahead of the Beatles or what your average Rapper might produce. Moreover it is a quintessentially Van Zandt County kind of manifesto, not to be denied, denounced, or denigrated.

There are gravestones, of course, that speak of wasted years, trashed talents, broken promises, crippling addictions, inhuman cruelties, deferred dreams, debilitating diseases, and bloody violence. Many of these came to rest here no doubt feeling like Socrates, unjustly condemned to death by lesser men, who told his friend, Crito, to sacrifice a rooster on the morning after he had drunk the hemlock to celebrate his release from "terrible life."

I will not linger in telling you of our young daughter's white marble marker with its somber words from Job 1:21, "The Lord has given. The Lord has taken away. Blessed be the name of the Lord." Nor will I wallow in maudlin sentimentality over the graves of my parents whose Texas red granite tombstone carries carvings of the irises that bloomed around our house, along with the proper names and the proper dates. They started married life together not a mile from here, Josie Helen Johnson and John Hardy Valentine; and after nearly sixty years together, they now rest here together side by side, and they will be rising together on that great Waking Up Morning. Is this shouting ground, or what?

All in all, this graveyard is a lovely place.

And it is not unlike untold thousands of other such places.

I think of Huntsville's secluded bower in a patch of dense East Texas woods where Sam Houston rests in peace by a Sidney Lanier poem carved in stone, "Into the woods my Master went. Clean forspent . . . ."

Stratford on Avon comes to mind with William Shakespeare's modest marker in a little graveyard by a small Anglican church, saying simply, "Good friend for Jesus' sake forebeare, to dig the dust enclosed here. Blest be the man that spares these stones, and curst be he that moves my bones."

I admire an old, old cemetery in old Mobile where giant live oaks laden with centuries-old accumulations of Spanish moss shelter the last resting places of the city's early settlers.

Secluded little hollows in the Great Smoky Mountains also come to mind, places on narrow dirt roads where little white church houses are twinned with neat little cemeteries on green hillsides with markers bearing old Anglo-Saxon names on stones long since so weathered and lichened that God only knows who they were, or when they were born, or when their travails ceased and their impossible dreams were put on hold.

A few hardy souls are still around who know the rigors of hard labor over row crops of cotton and corn, who experienced the broiling heat of the summer sun as backs were bent under the undulating heat waves that old folks called Lazy Lawrence, and who toiled at the tiresome task of chopping and hoeing which row crops demand. Those who remember that work will remember even more clearly the blessed relief that came when the work could be laid down for a few minutes and rest could be found in the shade at the end of the row. How delicious it is to sit in the shade for a little while, hat off, with a slight breeze blowing in the face, a long drink of cool water, and respite from the burning of the noonday heat and the burden of the day. Shade at the end of the row. It is a special dispensation of grace.

Is not the graveyard, for its occupants, this world's ultimate shade at the end of the row?

So, until death is finally swallowed up in victory for the people of God, it seems to me that it is not going to get any better than this, to rest in peace in the shade at the end of the row.

☙ Ich Glaube än Gott ❧

WHEN ADOLPH HITLER'S Nazi juggernaut was at the point of overrunning Bonn, Karl Barth made a big decision. Rather than bow the knee to the Nazi evil, Karl Barth chose to flee. Leaving his prestigious teaching post at the world-class University of Bonn, he made his way across the southern border of Germany to his native Switzerland where he enlisted as a private in the Swiss army and served until the war was finally over. Then he returned to his teaching post at the University of Bonn. The University buildings together with the quintessentially civilized city of Bonn had been bombed into smithereens by the conquering Allied Forces. Classes began in the rubble amidst the dust and noise, the hammering and screeching of heavy machinery, and all the commotion of massive reconstruction. Barth's first words to his first class in his first lecture on theology were, "Ich Glaube än Gott"—I believe in God.

What better way to begin again?

What better Christian testimony?

What better theology?

What better ethics?

What seems to me to be Karl Barth's Germanic circumlocutions in his portentous writings can be, at the very best, daunting. After being translated by scholars into English, they then need to be translated into my native East Texas language by non-academics who are able to communicate ideas without obfuscation, profundity without pedantry. These people must never, ever have studied German grammar, German verb forms, or German philosophers.

Still, Karl Barth is a great theologian whose contributions to the Christian cause must not be denied or denigrated or diminished. His memorable manifesto, "I believe in God," deserves to be immortalized, emblazoned on every believer's soul, highlighted in every Christian's everyday life, and used as a daily credo by the people of God everywhere.

Job said, "Though he slay me, yet will I trust him."

Paul said, "I am persuaded that neither death, nor life, nor angels, nor principalities, nor powers, nor things present, nor things to come, nor height, nor depth, nor any other creature, shall be able to separate us from the love of God, which is in Christ Jesus our Lord."

When the man whose son was grievously afflicted came to Jesus for deliverance, the Lord told him that all things are possible to those who believe. The father then cried out, "Lord, I believe; help thou my unbelief."

And Karl Barth just said, "I believe in God."

So what to do?

What to do when your Mother has just breathed her last breath and her pulse has stilled? "I believe in God."

What to do when the Medical Doctor says soberly, "I am sorry to have to tell you that the cancer has metastasized?" "I believe in God."

What to do when you drive around the corner and see that your house has burned, along with everything in it, to the ground? "I believe in God."

What to do when the phone rings at 1 o'clock in the morning and the voice from the Emergency Room at the hospital says, "Your son has been in a very bad automobile accident. You should come as quickly as possible"? "I believe in God."

What to do when the broker says that your retirement savings, painfully accumulated for all your working life have been wiped out? "I believe in God."

What to do when your spouse who decades ago stood with you happily and pledged, "Till death do us part," comes in one morning to say, "I am filing for divorce?" "I believe in God."

What to do when the child development specialist says, "This child can never see, or walk, or talk, or even hold a rattler?" "I believe in God."

What to do when the work Supervisor says, "I'm sorry, but your position has been eliminated and you have until 5 o'clock this afternoon to clear out your desk?" "I believe in God."

On the other hand, consider the other side of this coin.

What to do when a much hoped for position opens and you get the word that you have been chosen to fill it? "I believe in God."

What to do when the editor himself calls to say they like your manuscript very much, will publish it next Spring, and want a contract signed for your next two books? "I believe in God."

What to do when the incredibly wonderful young woman who has been the focus of your life for more than two years finally says "Yes?" "I believe in God."

What to do when a long and stressful pregnancy is succeeded by a very difficult delivery, but then the Medical Doctor emerges into the waiting room all bathed in smiles to announce, "You have a fine, healthy, beautiful baby girl?" "I believe in God."

Yes. In the bad times and in the good times, there is solid reason for the believer to affirm faith in God, to declare confidence in God, to confess dependence on God, to acknowledge reliance on God, to rest securely in the solid insight of Micah 6:8 that what the Lord requires of us is to do justice, to love mercy, and to walk humbly with our God.

When the storms of life are raging, God stands by his own.

When the challenging opportunities of a lifetime are presented, God moves to make his strength perfect in our weakness.

I believe in God.

But what is it to believe?

Here is where the water hits the wheel. Defining the word, believe, may very well take a lifetime of intellectual and spiritual struggle. The German word is *Glaube*. The Hebrew word is *aman*. The Greek word is *pisteuo*. The Spanish word is *creer*.

According to the Oxford English Dictionary, the best dictionary in the English language, our word believe is an ancient compounding of the verb "be" and the noun "life." Thus, believe means to be in life committed. The Christian believer is one who has consciously and positively, intentionally and wholeheartedly, decided to follow Jesus. No turning back. For the believer, there are no exceptions listed in fine print at the bottom of the contract. Jesus Christ is Lord. Period. Paragraph.

So, with Karl Barth, "Ich Glaube än Gott."

I believe in God.